Surviving My Son's Suicide

A Father's Perspective

STEVE SORENSEN

COPYRIGHT

ACKNOWLEDGMENT

I wish to express my sincere gratitude to David Gatewood for editing this book. He is a true gentleman and professional. If you are in need of great editor, look no further. David can be contacted at the following website.

http://lonetrout.com/

DEDICATION

*In loving memory of my beloved son Jeffrey Allen Sorensen.
Your life was too short, and I will forever miss you.*

October 10, 1991, to December 21, 2011.

*To my wife and two children Jessica and Joseph, I love you all
so very much. There is no way I could have come through this
ordeal without you. You have been my inspiration to get up
every day and keep living. My deepest regret is that you had to
suffer through the same anguish as me.*

*To the suicide support groups, Judi's House, and everyone else
who so patiently listened to me as I worked through the pain of
losing my son.*

INTRODUCTION

On December 21, 2011, my twenty-year-old son died suddenly and without any warning. His death was not caused by an illness, or an accident—Jeff's life was abruptly and violently ended by a self-inflicted gunshot wound. When the initial shock of his death wore off, and it finally registered in my mind that he was intentionally gone by his own hand, I doubted I would be able to live without him or with the truth that he really killed himself. My life had been destroyed beyond recognition, and in an instant our future was over. My son was gone forever.

I was consumed by guilt for having failed to save his life, and furious with him for having abandoned us in such a sudden and violent way. I felt a deep and dark despair permeating my whole being as I realized my son did not want the life my wife Stephanie and I had conceived together. It made me feel broken and defective. It made me feel as if something was wrong with me, because my child had lost the desire live.

Through this self-inflicted violent act, he not only ended his own life—he ended mine as well. When Jeff died, suicide was put on my radar and became a permanent and enduring part of my thought process. I now worry more than ever about my other surviving children and my wife. I no longer have the luxury of blindly trusting they will be okay, that they will not die suddenly. When any of them get upset or hurt, it terrifies me they might want to kill themselves too, an idea I had never entertained before Jeff's suicide.

After I had received the terrible news that my boy was gone forever, I spent the first three weeks in bed, crying every day, all day, until there were no tears left. I couldn't eat or sleep, and I was physically and emotionally ill. I began to wonder if a person could actually die from grief. This was the most painful emotional anguish I had ever experienced in my entire life. I exhausted myself by replaying the details of our last days and hours together in my mind. I was desperately searching for a reason to explain why my son felt there was no other alternative to suicide. In the end I came up with absolutely nothing to explain this horrific and senseless tragedy.

When I returned to work, I discovered everything had changed. The horrific events of the past few months had damaged my ability to perform my job. I was suffering from post-traumatic stress syndrome, and I was not able to concentrate or think. I couldn't focus on any task for more than a few minutes. I was sure I had completely lost my mind because of Jeff's death. Even remarkably straightforward assignments were too difficult for me, because my short-term memory was no longer functioning. I constantly wondered if normal daily activities were even still possible. For the first few months, I spent most of my workday staring at the computer, waiting until I could go home so I could lock myself in my bedroom and be alone. I felt totally disconnected from everyone and everything.

I couldn't think about work because I was too obsessed with my loss. The same questions kept rolling around in my mind over and over. What did I do wrong? How am I to go on living after this? What on earth am I going to do now? Why did you do this to yourself Jeff? I was trapped in a place where all I could ask was why.

Thankfully, over time the intensity of my emotions diminished somewhat. I regained the ability to function and get through the days and weeks without constant breakdowns, but I know I will mourn the loss of my son for the rest of my life. Although I continue to get out of bed every day and carry on with life, I don't feel the same amount of pleasure and passion for things that I used to. There is a hole in my heart that cannot be filled, and in this dark place, I feel only Jeff's constant and present absence. I deeply lament that Jeff will always be twenty years old in my mind, and I will never get to experience the privilege of seeing my son grow to adulthood. This tremendous burden of loss will never grow lighter; I can only hope for the strength to endure grief's enormous weight.

Stephanie and I wrote the following obituary after losing Jeff to suicide. This brief summary of his short life took days to write. It is something I never imagined doing for one of my children.

OBITUARY

Jeffrey Allen Sorensen, beloved son and brother, passed away unexpectedly on December 21, 2011. Jeff was born on October 10, 1991, and has been a source of pride to his family and friends since that day.

Jeff unconditionally loved his younger sister and brother, and took tremendous pride in being their older brother. He possessed a lifelong love of music and delighted in sharing this pleasure with others. Jeff was taken from us too soon and will always be loved and missed.

Jeff was proud to serve his country and his community. His service to the United States Navy as a Hospital Corpsman was among the proudest achievements of his life. Jeff also served his community and neighbors through volunteer work at the Parker Task Force. He was actively working to fulfill his aspirations of becoming a paramedic and performing emergency medicine to help those in need.

Jeff displayed courage and caring as a young man and always placed the feelings of others above his own. We will always love and miss you.

WELCOME TO YOUR LIFE

Stephanie and I had been married for several years before we thought about having a baby. Over time, we considered the possibility of starting a family more often, and after quite a bit of discussion we finally made a decision to go for it. Stephanie stopped taking her birth control pills, and within eight weeks she was pregnant with Jeff.

In the months leading to Jeff's birth, we did everything we could to ensure he would be a healthy baby: prenatal checkups, vitamins, exercise, you name it. I attended every well baby check that I possibly could, and beamed with pride when I first heard his heartbeat through the ultrasound. Stephanie was only 24 when he was born, so along with the wonders of modern medicine we had youth on our side.

Jeff was born on October 10, 1991, in the middle of the night, after a long and painful labor. In my humble opinion, he was a perfect baby; he had ten fingers, ten toes and gorgeous eyes that stared up at me with such a sense of wonderment and joy. I instantaneously fell in love with my new baby, and that feeling only grew every day.

Jeff was my first-born, and as any father would attest to, your first is particularly significant for several reasons. Every part of the experience is new, exciting, and terrifying all at the same time. I was replete with emotions unlike any I had felt before. I recall a tremendous sense of pride and an absolute joy for the privilege of being part of this miracle of life. At the same time, I felt a mind-boggling level of panic because, for better or worse, my life had changed forever. I was a father, and I would now be responsible for someone other than myself.

To me, a father has to be more than some old man sitting at the head of the dinner table. A father is a leader and a guide, who teaches his children things they will never learn in school. Like the value of hard work, and that your word is your honor. A father is a healer of bumps, bruises and broken hearts. A father protects his children from all the bad things in the world; he keeps his children from harm. He is a creator of homes and futures. A father is a dreamer. I dreamt of the days we would share together and of all the exciting things we would do together. Above everything else, my greatest desire was that my children would come home safely every day, and that their life would be filled with peace and happiness.

EARLY YEARS

After Jeff was born, I honestly believed that nothing could stop my family from realizing all of its dreams. Everything seemed so perfect. We had a new house, a new healthy baby boy, and I was moving up in my career. Stephanie and I were deeply in love with each other and with life. We knew we could raise the perfect child, because our negative childhood experiences had taught us what not to do. We had no clue there was such a grim future looming ahead us.

Jeff was an easy baby to care for because he was happy and healthy most of the time. He slept through the night by the time he was a few months old and he seemed to be quite intelligent and inquisitive. As a toddler he quickly mastered the ability to crawl, and he got into absolutely everything, which drove me crazy. None of our fragile possessions were safe. We had to put everything away because he would not be deterred from getting into things. His curiosity about the world drove him to discover everything around him. He was basically unstoppable. He also learned to walk and talk at an unusually early age. I was convinced I had a young genius on my hands. Stephanie and I were extremely proud of our wonderful baby.

The only things that ever concerned me seemed so inconsequential compared to all the great things Jeff was capable of. For example, unless he was sleeping he would not let me hold him, and if I tried he would arch his back and scream until I put him down. He was extremely active and would never sit still. He moved around the house like a Tasmanian devil. He never sat calmly and played with his toys. We couldn't put him in a stroller and go for walks—he absolutely couldn't tolerate being strapped in. Other experienced parents labeled him as "busy." I just wanted some peace and quiet once in a while.

At the time, I assumed this was normal behavior for a baby boy and did not give it too much thought. Overall I felt blessed, even though I was totally exhausted most of the time. In hindsight I now realize these were early warning signs.

THE NIGHTMARE

Not long after Jeff was born, I experienced a terrifying nightmare one cold winter night just before Christmas. Jeff's nursery was located at the end of the hallway on the second floor. The hallway was situated next to a loft that overlooked the first-floor family room. In this dream, I envisioned a massive, hairy-clawed hand reaching over the railing toward the door of the nursery. I stood by helplessly and watched as the dark gnarled hand opened Jeff's door and snatched him from his crib. I could see the terror in Jeff's eyes as the claw disappeared over the balcony, taking him away forever. I reached out for him, but I couldn't keep him from the demon. I immediately awoke screaming: A monster has Jeff!

I only had this dream one time, and I never had any nightmares like this about my other two children. Even though I tried to dismiss this dream, it continued to haunt me throughout Jeff's childhood.

Soon after Jeff died by suicide, I thought about the nightmare again. I began to believe it was more of a premonition than a dream, a premonition that now haunts my waking hours.

WARNING SIGNS

Stephanie endured an exceptionally difficult and emotionally abusive childhood. She was adopted by her parents when she was just a baby, for reasons we cannot explain because her family was so secretive about it. Her mother was cruel to her, and her father beat her. She was often told that she was unlovable and worthless. Her siblings were not adopted, and they were loved and adored by their parents, making Stephanie feel even worse.

By the time she was eighteen, she had grown intolerant of her parents' mistreatment of her, and decided to move out of their house. To suggest her parents were not supportive of the idea would be putting it mildly. As she was walking out of the front door for the last time, her mother said, "If you leave this house I will never speak to you again." At the time, Stephanie dismissed her mother's words as an angry threat, but her mother never forgave Stephanie for leaving, and refused to talk to her ever again. Ironically, both of her parents died of natural causes just weeks after Jeff died. She did not mourn their passing.

Because of her abusive childhood, Jeff was so vital to her. She wanted to prove to the world and herself that she could raise a wonderful loving boy. She was going to give Jeff everything she did not receive, and in return he would grow into a healthy and compassionate adult. Unfortunately, life rarely works according to plan.

Although Jeff was an easy baby, his behavior grew worse as each year passed. He was becoming exceptionally difficult to care for, because he was either extremely hyper or severely depressed. He had a remarkably short attention span, even for a child. When Jeff played with his toys, he would drop them in the middle of his room, play for a few minutes at most, and then dump something else out, and then something else. He never seemed able to focus his attention on anything for long. After all his worldly possessions were scattered everywhere, he would get bored, and then stop playing with them all together. These gargantuan messes could take an entire weekend to clean up. Every time we reorganized all the toys into bins, Jeff would dump everything back out again. We tried everything to get him to stop doing this, but nothing worked.

When Jeff was two years old, he received a cowboy outfit complete with holsters and shiny silver pop guns for Halloween. He had an entirely insatiable obsession with guns. He only wanted to play with guns, guns and more guns. He was driving us totally crazy with the gun thing. One morning Jeff walked up to Stephanie, pulled one of the fake revolvers from his holster and pistol-whipped her while she was on the toilet. This was a colossal mistake for Jeff. Stephanie was furious, and had a lump on her head to go with the anger. All of Jeff's toy guns were thrown in the trash, and he was told he would never receive another toy gun again. He went into a deep depression and begged for a new gun, but the pistol whipping had been the last straw. He no longer wanted to play with any other toys, and his obsession deepened even further. Later he would improvise and make Lego rifles and pistols that he would use to defend the home to keep the monsters at bay. When Legos were not available, Jeff would use sticks instead. There seemed to be no way to stop him from obsessing over guns.

Jeff also struggled in school and daycare because he was unable to control his impulses. Whatever thought popped into his mind, he would act on it, no matter how inappropriate the idea was. He was always being disciplined for this impulsiveness, but there were no consequences severe enough to change the behavior. These impulse-control issues grew worse and worse, and our marriage began to show signs of strain. Stephanie was thoroughly exasperated with Jeff since nothing she tried was successful. She often lost her patience and her temper after long bouts of trying to get Jeff to cooperate or behave. She frequently channeled her frustration into me at the end of the day, causing more arguments than I care to remember. Looking back, it was as though there was a pain raging inside him, a hurt he did not know how to relieve or manage. He was not an easy child to love or take care of. Just when you thought you had won him over, and won his trust, he would lash out against you.

Soon daycares, schools and friends were unwilling to deal with Jeff. I cannot begin to count the number of times I was called into the principal's or the day care director's office for his misbehavior, or the number of late-night discussions Stephanie and I had related to our aggravation with him. He was never in harmony with what was going on around him, or what other people were doing. Before long Jeff's behavior was the only topic of conversation Stephanie and I had shared.

One occasion that comes to mind was when we needed a babysitter on short notice so Stephanie and I could fly to Steamboat Springs on a friend's private plane. This was such an extraordinary opportunity we desperately wanted to go. After a great deal of searching and begging, I was finally able to talk a friend at work into watching him. On the day of the flight, we dropped Jeff and our baby girl Jessie off at my friend's house and went on our adventure. I recall my friend and his wife were excited to babysit because they were planning to start a family and they wanted to experience what it was like. Jeff was eight and my daughter Jessie was two, so the idea was that she would watch our baby girl, and he would hang out with Jeff. What could go wrong? When we returned to pick up the kids, I could clearly see the look of frustration and anger I so often witnessed with daycare providers, teachers and Stephanie. "Jessie was an absolute joy to take care of, but..."

I soon discovered that they had taken Jeff to the store to get some food for lunch. While they were shopping, Jeff ran through the store, out of control, pulling items off the shelves and throwing them on the ground. They left the store utterly humiliated and walked out to their car in the adjacent parking lot. While they were getting Jessica buckled into her car seat, Jeff urinated all over the vehicle. When they arrived back home, Jeff went wild, breaking things in the house. At lunchtime, he poured ketchup all over the floor and threw food. I was embarrassed and angry. This was not new information for us. Jeff simply couldn't control his impulses, and there were no workable techniques to cajole him into behaving properly.

Over time, we learned how to shelter Jessie—and later Joey, my youngest—from all the drama and conflict that went on, in large part due to our failure to get Jeff under control. Although Jeff could be an absolute terror, and break every rule I could set, he was loving and kind to his siblings. Jessie and Joey positively adored their older brother, and that is exactly how I wanted it to be. I suspected Jeff had a disability, but I did not want to burden our children with adult issues or damage their opinion of him. Jeff was cycling between mania and depression most of the time, but when he was not in trouble he was a pleasant and loving child.

DIAGNOSIS

Many people blamed Jeff's hyperactivity, depression and lying on our inability to parent him properly. Most people would offer anecdotal advice when we would complain about his behavior. I was told so many times that if I just changed my approach, Jeff would behave. The truth is we tried everything, but absolutely nothing worked. Jeff would cycle between high and low moods several times per day, driving everyone around him to utter distraction. He continued to get into trouble with his teachers at school and with his mom at home. He would wear out his welcome within minutes no matter what the situation.

During a long train ride to Chicago when Jeff was eight years old, he told Stephanie he often thought about killing himself. This new revelation terrified her and immediately prompted us to seek professional help for him. When she returned from the trip, she scheduled him for a psychiatric evaluation at the University of Colorado. During his assessment, Jeff told the doctors he had dreams about monsters biting him and tearing out his tendons and muscles. He then went on to tell them he had thoughts about killing himself to stop these nightmares permanently. These new revelations finally got the attention we needed to help Jeff. He underwent multiple evaluations, but we discovered childhood mood disorders could be quite difficult to diagnose. Some doctors thought Jeff was hyper, or he was suffering from Attention Deficit Hyperactivity Disorder (ADHD); others thought it was our parenting approach. Jeff lied so often it made the diagnosis even harder to achieve. After many interviews, he was eventually diagnosed with bipolar disorder.

We learned the first manic or depressive episode of bipolar disorder generally occurs in the teenage years or early adulthood. Jeff was only eight years old when he was diagnosed. Many people with bipolar disorder are overlooked or misdiagnosed, resulting in unnecessary suffering, because the symptoms can be subtle and complex. Neither Stephanie nor I was prepared for the difficult challenges a bipolar child presents.

Bipolar disorder is characterized by vacillating episodes of mania and depression. In extreme cases, during a manic period some patients can have a complete break from reality. This helped to clarify Jeff's fear of monsters and his obsession with guns as a means of defense.

Another symptom, hypomania, is defined as a high-energy state in which a person feels exuberant but doesn't lose their grip on reality. Jeff found this state to be thoroughly enjoyable because his mood was elevated, and he had an immense amount of energy. When he was experiencing this extreme euphoria and hypomania, he would get into trouble at home, or in school. The adults who were charged with supervising or teaching Jeff certainly did not appreciate his extremely disruptive energy. During hypomania, Jeff had an inflated self-esteem and did not consider the consequences of his actions. He did not recognize or acknowledge that his mind was racing out of control—he just acted out.

The inability to focus on one activity for very long is another classic symptom of bipolar disorder. People who can harness this energy when they are in a hypomanic condition can be highly productive. Jeff was one of those unlucky people who would go from task to task, never finishing before moving on to something else. His schoolwork reflected this inability to concentrate. He was dubbed the class clown because he acted out and made people laugh, rather than doing his assigned tasks.

Conversely, when he left the manic state he would exhibit symptoms of classic depression. Everyone has off days from time to time, but in people with bipolar disorder it becomes so powerful it interferes with their ability to function. Jeff would descend into feelings of sadness and hopelessness that he couldn't escape. The interesting thing to me was that Jeff never threatened to kill himself since his original diagnosis, even when he was very depressed, but he would mope around the house in a deep depression for days or weeks at a time for no apparent reason. I used to mistakenly believe he was just feeling sorry for himself.

Bipolar and lying go hand in hand for most manic-depressives. During episodes of mania, the brain is out of rational control, and whatever pops up spews out of the mouth, which in most cases turns out to be lies. In addition, Jeff often experienced hallucinations. Mostly these were voices no one but him experienced. Jeff's reality was different from ours, so many times he was just telling us what he believed he experienced. I also believe he thought nothing of telling outrageous stories when they served his purpose, or enhanced his image somehow.

Although the causes of bipolar disorder are not fully understood, it often runs in families. My younger sister is cognitively delayed and suffers from the problem, and even though my father was never officially diagnosed I believe he is afflicted with the disorder as well.

According to the American Foundation for Suicide Prevention, ninety percent of people who kill themselves have a diagnosable and treatable psychiatric ailment like clinical depression, bipolar disorder, or some other depressive illness. With proper treatment and support, we were assured Jeff could live a normal and fulfilling life.

Unfortunately for Jeff this was not to be. What I did not understand at the time was that bipolar is a life-threatening disease and it is even more serious when manifested at an early age in children. My unwillingness to accept or understand how serious this disease really was continues to haunt me to this day. I did not understand then that we were fighting for his survival, nor did I ever understand how high the odds were that I would not win that battle.

There is no denying the fact that it is difficult, raising a child with bipolar disease. There are times when you need to scream, days when you think you can't take it anymore, weeks when you know you haven't made a difference in their life, and moments when you want to turn your back on them. It is their problem, not yours, and yet it becomes yours since you love the person suffering from the disease. You have no choice: you must stand by your child. You are caught in the disease as surely as they are. You will hate the disease at times, hate what it does to your life, your marriage, your own sanity. Hate it or not, you are the parent, and whatever it takes, you have to make it work somehow.

TREATMENT PLAN

As of this writing, there is no known cure for bipolar disorder—there are only treatments that can help people achieve better control of their mood swings and related symptoms. Because bipolar disorder is a lifelong and chronic disease, people need long-term medical care to control the symptoms. An effective maintenance treatment plan includes medicine and psychotherapy for preventing recurrence and decreasing symptom severity. Jeff was eventually placed into this type of treatment plan.

Typically, a psychiatrist is required to prescribe bipolar medications. Since not everyone responds to medications in the same way, a number of diverse prescriptions may need to be tried before the best course of treatment is discovered. Blood levels have to be monitored to establish the right dose for the patient. This is an unpleasant roller coaster ride for everyone involved. Along with the blood tests, parents are asked to keep a record of daily moods, sleep patterns, and life events to assist the doctors in tracking and treating the condition effectively.

Jeff was eventually prescribed lithium, which was the original mood-stabilizing medicine approved by the

U.S. Food and Drug Administration (FDA) in the 1970s for treatment of manic disorder. This drug is meant to control symptoms of mania and prevent the recurrence of depressive episodes. Jeff hated being on lithium. He said it made him feel sluggish and numb. He also experienced side effects, including hand tremors, nausea and itching skin. He strenuously resisted taking the medication even though it was effectively stabilizing his mood swings. The best and worst of the lithium was how normal it made him feel. The danger there is what happens to most manic-depressives who take lithium. At some point, they decide they are fine, cured, and no longer need it.

In the end, his medication gave us yet another thing to argue over. He lied about taking the lithium and skipped doses frequently, causing wild fluctuations of his blood levels. As a result, the doctors treating Jeff had an extremely difficult time prescribing the appropriate dose, resulting in even more issues. We could never persuade Jeff to cooperate with his treatment plan.

TREATMENT FAILURE

Although someone might be willing to believe they have bipolar disorder, they may not be willing to endure the prescribed treatment. It is almost impossible to force a person to take medication if they don't want to accept treatment. Unless he or she is committed to a medical facility, is under legal guardianship, or is legally required to comply with a doctor's recommendations, they can lawfully refuse. When Jeff was younger, we tried to make him accept treatment; however, by the age of sixteen he was legally allowed to advocate for himself and refuse treatment, which is exactly what he chose to do. We all knew it was only a matter of time before disaster struck him. We just did not know what form it would take. There was no amount of begging or threatening that would make him continue treatment. He said he felt fine, the lithium had cured him, and he no longer needed it. This was typical behavior for a manic-depressive. To make matters worse, the psychiatrist we were paying to treat Jeff supported his decision. Stephanie and I were in a complete state of shock when we discovered we had no authority to override this absurd decision. To this day, we are convinced this was one of the key factors leading to Jeff's suicide.

Jeff opted to go off medication because he wanted to recapture the feeling of euphoria he used to feel. And once he'd totally abandoned treatment, the old thoughts and behaviors associated with his mental illness returned with a vengeance. He ultimately decided he did not need medication ever again. His manically-driven euphoric self-confidence had caused him to conclude that the only reason he was medicated was because we wanted to control him.

However, Jeff was not able to deal with his bipolar symptoms without help. He began to self-medicate with drugs and alcohol in a desperate attempt to relieve his pain. Jeff was not unusual in his approach. In 1996, Dr. Kathleen Brady reported at the U.S. Psychiatric and Mental Health Congress that thirty to sixty percent of people with bipolar disorder also have issues with drug or alcohol abuse. Dr. Brady also stated that substance abuse is more likely to occur in people with bipolar disorder than in people with other psychiatric disorders, such as compulsive eating, schizophrenia or anxiety disorders.

From a bigger-picture perspective, Dr. Agnes B. Hatfield says up to fifty percent of people with mental illnesses also struggle with abuse of substances like drugs and alcohol. Jeff began to suffer serious substance-abuse problems, particularly alcohol abuse, after he stopped taking his prescriptions. He got drunk when he was manic to enhance the rush of his euphoria, or to improve his mood when he was depressed. What he did not realize was alcohol, in fact, depresses the brain. He was making his depression worse than it already was.

We knew Jeff was in trouble and we were fundamentally incapable of stopping his self-destructive behavior. Not only could we not stop the impulsive behaviors, and the drinking: we couldn't prevent him from taking his life. I faulted the medical community for allowing Jeff to advocate for himself, I blamed his friends for getting him the drugs and alcohol, and I blamed the person who sold him the gun he used to kill himself with. However, I ultimately placed most of the blame on myself, because it seemed inconceivable my love for Jeff was not strong enough to keep him alive. I was his father. I should have been able to protect him from his demons. I always believed that loving Jeff enough would make a difference, or help, or maybe even cure him. It couldn't cure him, but never for a single instant of his life did he doubt that I cared about him.

Years later I eventually came to accept that I was not to blame for Jeff's death. He never sought my permission to kill himself, and if he had I would not have approved. I finally had to accept that it was Jeff's decision to complete suicide, and all I can do is disagree with his decision.

FALLING OUT

There were many arguments from the moment Jeff turned eighteen. He wanted everything to be different for him, and it wasn't. It couldn't be. He was emotionally young for his age, and had the same poor impulse control he'd always had, which was barely held in check by his medications when he decided to take them.

Jeff also continued to lie about anything and everything, and it was quite exhausting playing detective with him all the time. I was always trying to figure out what was true and what was fiction. He was constantly engaging in self-destructive impulsive behavior and getting into trouble. He had improved when he was taking his medication, but he deteriorated once he stopped, and my patience with him had worn exceedingly thin. I did not know how to deal with his defiant behavior and I feared I was losing control of the situation. We spent all of our energy on Jeff and practically ignored the other children. I did not want him to influence my younger children in a negative way, and I did not want them sacrificed to him and his disease. Things were coming to a head, and we all knew it. The final straw for us was the discovery of Jeff's stash of alcohol, cigarettes, and drugs.

Jeff was never a boy who loved to play outside. He preferred the chaos of his room, and he especially hated being cold or dirty. However, he started to feel a newfound love of nature walks. After dinner, he would often announce he needed to go hiking to relax and blow off some steam. This was so uncharacteristic of him that we were becoming highly suspicious, so eventually Stephanie decided to follow his trail. The recent snowfall made it extremely easy to retrace his recent footsteps to a grotto near our home. When she arrived at the end of the makeshift path the freshly fallen snow had created, she discovered a treasure trove of alcohol, cigarettes and drug paraphernalia. Much to our dismay, we discovered these walks had been an excuse to get intoxicated, smoke cigarettes or get high. Along with this new evidence, we were convinced he had been driving while under the influence of alcohol. We decided to crack down and take away his driving privileges before he ended up with a DUI or worse.

The day we found his stash, Stephanie and I drove down to the local movie theatre where Jeff worked to pick him up. On the drive home, we confronted Jeff about our suspicions and, on cue, he lied about everything. When we finally disclosed to him that we had discovered the secret stash, he admitted he had indeed been drinking, and smoking. When I told him we would not accept this type of behavior in our home, he replied by saying he would just move out the house, since he was eighteen. I thought he was bluffing because he had nowhere to go, but I was wrong.

The following Friday, Jeff skipped school and took off with some of his friends. When we went to pick him up from school, he was nowhere to be found. We tried texting and calling him several times, but received no response. We tried to reach him all weekend, but we were met with the same silence. Finally, on Sunday night he replied by text that he was okay, and that we should not worry about him. He then went on to say that he found a girl willing to let him move in with her and her divorced mother.

Jeff and the girl showed up on Monday. He packed all of his belongings into garbage bags and loaded them into her car. The whole time this was going on, Stephanie was unable to watch what was happening because of her similar experience with her parents. When the last of Jeff's things were loaded, I asked him to at least say goodbye to Stephanie, so we all sat down at the kitchen table. Stephanie started by saying he should not leave because she was confident we could work this out. Jeff was entirely unmoved, which brought Stephanie to absolute tears. Upon seeing this, I became tremendously angry and shouted "Look at what this is doing to us!" He calmly looked at me and said, your anger is exactly why I'm leaving. His response completely surprised me because I was typically an extraordinarily patient person, and rarely lost my temper. I looked at him in shock, and then he stood up and walked out the front door. Stephanie did not want a repeat of what had happened to her when she was eighteen, so she ran out the door after him and told him he was always welcome in our home. I sat at the kitchen table with my head in my hands and cried.

Jeff fell out of touch for the next few months. The automated attendance line called daily, informing us he had skipped some, or all, of his classes. We told the school he had moved out on his own, and there was nothing we could do, but the calls kept coming anyway. I was terribly concerned about him completing high school, let alone all the other problems I envisioned.

Jeff had become a hero to his classmates. The idea that he could walk out of the house, and tell his parents to shove it, absolutely amazed his friends. He constantly bragged about his adventures on Facebook. The only reason we knew anything about him is because he never bothered to "un-friend" us after he left home.

Probably the most hurtful thing Jeff did during this time away was agree to join the family for Mother's Day at a favorite local restaurant and then not show up. Stephanie was so very hopeful that this meal and time together would restart communication, and possibly allow us to improve the relationship. We sat in the restaurant for over two hours waiting; he never showed. I was furious beyond words, and my other children were deeply hurt. Mother's Day has never been the same since.

Because Stephanie spent most of her time worrying about Jeff, her health began to decline. She fell into a deep depression and suffered from severe insomnia. I was suffering from outrage. I couldn't believe my son was capable of such selfish, outrageous behavior. While our family was disintegrating, Jeff was voted Prom King and managed to graduate with a straight D average. He was elated with himself.

PSEUDO GRADUATION

In yet another attempt to fix the relationship with Jeff, Stephanie wanted to go to his high school graduation and then take him out to dinner to celebrate. I knew this was the right thing to do, but my heart simply was not in it. Jeff had slacked off for the last six months and destroyed our trust. How on earth was I going to go out to dinner with him and celebrate? It felt so hypocritical to me. I wondered what kind of example this was setting for my other two children. Would they idolize Jeff as his classmates did? Would they want to copy his behavior? In the end, the only reason I went was because I did not want to hurt Stephanie any more than she had already been.

We watched Jeff graduate from the bleachers. He staggered onto the podium, looking downright intoxicated as he accepted his diploma to wild cheers from his friends and their parents; he was a hero to them. We were not cheering. We probably were the only people in the entire stadium not cheering and clapping. I was seething with anger and disappointment. I had looked forward to this day since Jeff came into the world, and now he had completely ruined the experience for me and the rest of the family.

Afterward we went to a park and took pictures. Stephanie put her arms around his shoulders, and asked me to move in close so our daughter could take a picture of the three of us. I was not able to comply; instead I stood off to the side with my arms crossed, and a large angry scowl on my face. What I wanted to do at that moment was to punch him in the stomach, for causing the family so much pain.

After pictures, I suffered through a meal at his favorite restaurant. The whole time, I could only focus on how much he had hurt Stephanie on Mother's Day, and now we were there supporting him. Stephanie was trying so hard to connect with Jeff, and the other two kids were just happy to be with him. From my perspective, I felt Jeff was being totally insincere, and I couldn't be a part of it. It felt like another lie, a painful lie I couldn't deal with at the time. We finally finished the meal and then said our goodbyes. Stephanie cried the whole way home. I was driving, so I gripped the wheel with both hands and gritted my teeth. Several weeks would pass by before we would hear from Jeff again.

THE EMERGENCY ROOM

I was driving to work when my cell phone started ringing. Because of Jeff's recent behavior I was in a relatively poor mood, so I decided not to respond and let it go to voicemail. The phone started ringing again immediately. I figured it must be important, so I answered this time. Stephanie was calling to tell me Jeff had been in a fight, and his girlfriend's mother had taken him to the emergency room. She asked if I would stop by before going to work to make sure he was all right. I reluctantly agreed, and told her I would call when I found out what was going on.

When I got to the hospital, I found Jeff sitting in the waiting room. He had a black eye, broken nose and a fat lip. I asked him what happened, and he said someone punched him in the face for no reason whatsoever. I was sure this was yet another lie, but I let it go. I figured this was neither the time nor the place to start another argument. I started to ask him if he would like me to take him to the family doctor, when the woman sitting next to him said in a particularly nasty tone, "Aren't you even going to introduce yourself?" I had not noticed her sitting there, but when she spoke I assumed she was the girlfriend's mother. My first thought was, how could she allow Jeff to move in with her teenage daughter? Second, how could she have not called to talk to us about what was going on? Third, why was she being so rude toward me since she was to blame for allowing Jeff to get hurt?

Three months of repressed emotions were starting to boil to the surface. All I could say was, "No, I'm not going to introduce myself to you!" I wanted absolutely nothing to do with this woman. As far as I was concerned, she was as much to blame for all of this as Jeff was. I decided to ignore her completely. I then looked at Jeff and said, "Son, you have a choice to make right here and right now: you either leave with me, or stay with her." He glanced over to the woman I call "The Creature" and then to me. I was sure he was going to say goodbye to her and then walk out with me, but instead he took her hand and said, "I am staying with Mom."

What the hell did he say? I couldn't believe what I had just heard. My head felt as if it were going to explode. I had to get out of the hospital as quickly as possible. I practically ran out of the emergency room, jumped into the Jeep and drove off screaming and pounding the steering wheel. I had a full-blown, old-fashioned temper tantrum. Months of anger and rage were pouring out of me like a volcano. The level of betrayal I had witnessed was beyond anything I had ever imagined in my wildest dreams. How could he call someone else Mom? Stephanie had spent the last months in agony because her baby boy was gone, she barely functioned without him at home. Jeff was all she thought or cared about at the time; she was overcome with worry. She would give anything to get him back, to make him happy, and yet Jeff discarded her as easily as you might discard a torn shirt.

By some miracle, I was able to drive to work without getting into an accident. I parked the car outside of the building and called Stephanie. I thoroughly unloaded on her. After we both yelled and screamed and cried, I was finally able to calm down enough to hang up and go into work. Neither of us could believe what Jeff had just done to the family.

Not long after Jeff received his beating, he called his real mother and said he was leaving for the Navy, and he wanted to say goodbye. Stephanie called me at work to share this news. I was sure the Navy would not accept a person with bipolar disease. I assumed this must be another tall tale. She assured me he was serious and asked if I would be willing to meet for dinner so we could talk to him. I agreed, because I wanted him back, regardless of the pain he had inflicted on the family. Besides, I still wanted to punch him in the stomach.

FIRST HOMECOMING

We met at a small Italian restaurant in our neighborhood. I was the last one to arrive because I had to drive through rush-hour traffic from work. Stephanie and Jeff were already sitting in a booth waiting for me. It looked like they were engaged in a nice conversation. When I sat down I noticed Jeff still had some mild bruising on his face, but other than that there was no permanent damage from his fight. I was relieved to see he was okay. After I ordered something to drink, Jeff began to explain his phone call. He said he had been to see the Navy recruiter earlier that week, and they had openings for him right away. If things went according to plan, he would be shipping out to basic training within two days. Stephanie and I are both ex-military, so I did not have an issue with him wanting to serve his country; my issue was the bipolar. I asked him if he disclosed his medical history to the recruiter, and he answered yes. I seriously doubted he was being honest with me—I thought this was yet another lie. As usual, I let it go. We talked some more about his plans and then we agreed to all meet at the recruiter's office the next morning.

The following morning at the Naval Recruiting office I talked to the recruiter, and he seemed to be highly impressed with Jeff. I then asked him about the military accepting people with a prior diagnosis of bipolar. He looked surprised and said the Navy would not accept a person with mental illness. I knew Jeff had lied, and it looked as though I had spoiled his chance for joining the Navy. I still thought this was better than him getting caught later, and getting into even more trouble.

The recruiter called Jeff into his office to talk to him privately. I was thinking Jeff would never forgive me, but I honestly had his best interest in mind. After a short discussion in the office, the two of them emerged, and Jeff had a gigantic smile on his face. Apparently he'd convinced the recruiter he was not bipolar. He assured them he could pass any acceptance criteria they could throw at him. All I could say was "huh." The truth is that HIPPA protects an individual's past, present and future physical or mental health conditions, so Jeff did not have to disclose his history. It would be up to the Navy to disqualify him through a series of examinations.

As I expected, Jeff failed the first series of examinations, but it was not due to any mental-illness issues. His system was loaded with THC; Jeff had been smoking marijuana over the past few months and failed the drug test miserably. The recruiter suggested that Jeff should come back in six weeks and take the test again. Jeff would need some time in a proper environment to detox his system. This is how we persuaded him to move back in with us. He would be able to get cleaned up at home and then join the Navy.

When Jeff returned home with us, Stephanie and the children were thrilled. I was happy to have him home safe too, but I was still terribly upset with him. I knew we had a lot of work to do to repair our relationship. I was willing to let the past go, but I was not sure if Jeff's intentions were honorable or not. He lied so frequently it had become nearly impossible for me to believe anything he said. I did not want him to hurt me or the family any more than he already had.

While he was away, he had some scrapes with local law enforcement. The Navy was aware of these issues, and Jeff had to get everything settled in court, and pay any fines, before he could join. It turned out these court costs were more than one thousand dollars. Also, when he moved out he took many of his expensive electronics and other gifts we had given him through the years. When he came home, he had a grocery sack containing one change of unwashed clothes. He told us everything he owned had been stolen, but I'm sure he traded his belongings for drugs. Jeff had no money left, so I had to pay all of his legal bills, and buy him new clothes.

For the next several weeks while Jeff was waiting to get into the Navy, Stephanie and Jeff worked exceptionally hard on repairing their relationship. This was a particularly significant time for the two of them, and I was extremely pleased to see Stephanie begin to recover from the anxiety and despair she had suffered while Jeff was running wild. My experience was different. I was still catching Jeff lying to me, and I wondered what his intentions were. I adopted a wait-

and-see attitude. Jeff would have to work very hard to win my trust back.

LEAVING FOR THE NAVY

The weeks passed extremely quickly, and it was clear Jeff was trying his absolute hardest to put his past behind him. We had tons of chores for him to do every day as a form of repayment, and he completed all of them without complaint. He also volunteered in the community with his mother twice a week. We did not allow him to drive, drink or smoke. Since he had every intention of joining the Navy, he did not resume taking any medication for bipolar either. I began to think the diagnosis might have been a mistake, because he exhibited zero symptoms of the disease—or maybe he had outgrown it after all.

After several failed attempts, Jeff finally passed the recruiter's drug screen, and he officially signed an agreement to become a Naval Reservist. Despite some misgivings about him being in the reserves rather than full time, I was immensely proud of him. Jeff was going to be a Navy corpsman after all.

The day finally arrived: it was time for Jeff to leave for basic training. We drove him to the Military Entrance Processing Station in Denver. We were allowed to see him swear in, and then it was time to say goodbye, again. This experience was much better than the first goodbye, but it still hurt to see him go. He was finally becoming a respectable young man; all the years of struggle and sacrifice seemed to be paying off.

We soon discovered that Jeff was made for the military for several reasons. One, he still loved guns; two, the discipline kept him on the straight and narrow; and three, he was happier than he had ever been. During basic training, he was able to call and write, and he always sounded positive. I was becoming more convinced than ever he was not bipolar; he only needed the right environment to thrive in.

SECOND HOMECOMING

Jeff completed basic training and immediately started Navy A-School in Chicago. Since he was contracted to become a Navy corpsman, his training would focus on basic principles and techniques of patient care and first-aid procedures. To my surprise, Jeff excelled in all aspects of his training. No more class clown, and no more skipping classes. For the first time since he was a young boy, I had something to brag about.

Upon graduation, Jeff returned home again. He moved into the basement and began transitioning back into the family. Since he was now an adult and a Navy corpsman, we decided to treat him with the respect he had earned. We removed curfews and all other restrictions. He was extremely courteous and caused no issues. He helped around the house, and was generally a true joy to be around. But I could tell he missed being out on his own. I understood because I would have had a hard time moving back into my parents' house after being on my own for nearly a year. Therefore, it was no surprise when Jeff announced that he was moving out again.

Jeff decided to rent a small room in a house shared by three other people, one of them a Navy corpsman from his base. I thought it was a wonderful idea and I fully approved. Stephanie was not so excited. She still worried about him, but Jeff and I assured her over and over this was how it was supposed to be. She reluctantly agreed, and finally Jeff had her blessing to move out.

MOVING OUT AGAIN

The day had finally arrived, and it was time for Jeff to move out again. We spent the entire morning filling my five-by-ten trailer with all of his belongings, some of my old furniture, a few kitchen appliances, and an Olympic weight set. By the time we were finished loading everything the trailer was bursting at the seams.

To help him get off to a fresh start, I decided to give him the car he had used in high school. I wanted to show Jeff I trusted him and supported his decision to be more independent. I desperately wanted this move to be a positive experience for everyone so I could erase the negative memories from the first move. In hindsight, I realize I was being overzealous because I knew deep in my heart Jeff was not ready to be on his own.

As we were preparing to drive to his new home, Stephanie noticed the brake lights were out on the trailer we had spent the morning loading. I tried to figure out why they were not working, but I had no luck in isolating the problem. I knew it was getting ready to rain, and I did not want to have to deal with the aggravation of moving on another day. I wanted to take a chance and drive the stuff over without brake lights. Stephanie was emphatic we delay the move until the lights were fixed, but neither Jeff nor I wanted to deal with the delay. I asked her to follow me in her car, and watch for hand signals, but she hated the idea. Stephanie sat down on the front steps and refused to leave. She said she would not be a part of this madness. We argued over the brake lights for a quite a while, but she finally acquiesced. I knew she was decidedly unhappy with my solution, but we pressed on in spite of her misgivings. After an exceptionally long and slow drive, we safely arrived at Jeff's new house and helped him unload the trailer. When he was somewhat settled, we had some iced tea together and then said goodbye again.

Stephanie cried for most of the trip home, and confessed she had an unusually unpleasant feeling about Jeff being on his own. She thought the brake lights were a sign he should not move out, but she knew she would never be able to talk Jeff out of leaving. I also had some doubts, but I was so happy for him to have his own place I dismissed my concerns. I assumed this was how things were meant to be, and I did not want to stand in the way of his happiness.

What we did not know was that Jeff had arranged to buy a Smith & Wesson .45 caliber handgun just a few days after he moved out. Buying this weapon was something he'd always wanted to do, and he spent all of his money to fulfill this fantasy. In fact, most of his motivation for moving out was related to buying this gun. According to his roommates, he totally obsessed over his deadly new device. All the constraints and rules we placed on him when he was growing up were now lifted, and he was free to act out every gun fantasy he ever had. He spent all of his time playing with this lethal weapon as if it were a toy. On numerous occasions, he got intoxicated and fired the weapon in the back yard, trying to kill the neighborhood squirrels. The neighbors complained to the police multiple times, but when Jeff was questioned he would simply lie and say he didn't have a gun, and he didn't know where the gunshots were coming from. He always kept the gun loaded, and even slept with it under his pillow. His roommates were alarmed by his behavior but never said anything to us about it. Jeff never mentioned buying the gun to us because he knew we would have been extremely worried and he did not want us to spoil his fun.

Jeff only survived for three months before he finally killed himself with his gun. I'm reasonably sure his suicide was a compulsive action rather than a premeditated one, but the result is the same: Jeff is dead. The painful truth is, I will never know if he was depressed and in pain, or if he was just acting out of impulse because he was never able to share his true feelings with me. He was off his medications for nearly two years, and nearly fooled everyone. He hid his disease from the world so he could appear to be normal. Jeff only let others see what he wanted them to see— most people had no idea that he was in so much pain. He tried very hard to move through the last few months of his life with grace, despite the handicaps he was born with.

I continue to have a tremendous amount of guilt for letting Jeff talk me into moving out. I often think this decision was the final catalyst for his demise because he would have never pulled any of these stunts while living at home.

I have worn myself down trying to figure out why my beautiful and intelligent boy decided to take his own life. I had no understanding why this unthinkable choice had been made. I searched for answers, for reasons, for justification I was never to find. Sadly, the solution may never be clear to me. The reasons behind why a person would decide to take their own life are rarely clear. Some believe those who want to end their own life are doing so with a sound mind, free of mental illness or distress, and they are capable of making rational, well thought-out decisions. Attempting to understand exactly the logical process of the suicide victim is much like trying to learn a foreign language by listening in on a conversation. I could examine the sounds and syllables forever and a day, but it was not likely I was going to follow much of what was said.

Considering the accounts of those who have attempted suicide and lived to talk about it, we know the main goal of a suicide is not to end life, but to stop pain. Those in the vice-like grip of a self-destructive clinical depression are in emotional pain so intense it makes dying seem like a less objectionable option than living. One survivor likened the sensation to being at the bottom of a deep, black hole, and rather than fighting to get out, he wanted to burrow deeper into the depths. He said you can't even trust your own thoughts.

Even though suicide is not our choice, our lives are irreversibly affected by its consequences. I tried to imagine what I would have to suffer to make the same choice, and when I imagined Jeff in that level of pain it was almost too much to consider. However, there was a flaw in my thinking process. I was envisioning what suicidal depression looked like through my eyes, the eyes of a rational, healthy mind. Jeff had a distorted view of his world. Problems that seem solvable to me probably seemed impossible to him. His pain was amplified beyond reason, and death appeared to offer the only possible relief to his pain. Instead of being a "last resort," the severely depressed person may consider suicide as a reasonable "Plan B." This skewed vision has wisely described suicide as a permanent "solution" to a temporary problem.

Depressed subjects often give up taking antidepressants when the advantageous effects begin to kick in, just as bipolar patients stop taking lithium. This tendency may be caused by a fear of drug dependency, but some hypothesize it comes from a mortal terror of having to face the world now that a means for doing so has been provided. The pathological condition is preferable to the remedy.

Unfortunately, the vast majority of suicides result from untreated, mistreated, or unsuccessfully treated mental illness. The embarrassment surrounding mental illness or depression can present a barrier to healing and possibly result in suicide. Many people that are afflicted with mental illness don't want to admit to having issues, and many that do acknowledge the disease don't wish to tackle the problems. My son certainly fell into this category. The hopelessness felt by the person with thoughts of suicide, and the urgent need they feel to keep such feelings and thoughts secret, is another crucial issue. The person may feel unable to take any course but suicide to ease their mental anguish. Since they often feel they have no other option, is suicide their fault? For some survivors even being able to identify the reasons for a loved one's suicide is not enough to lessen their confusion and self-doubt.

As an outside observer, we can clearly see many other alternatives to death, but to the irrational mind there may be no other course of action to achieve release from suffering. Most suicides result from a disease that robs the victim of their ability to see any other choice but death. They certainly did not ask for the illness, and they did not understand or select the consequences of having the disease. We don't blame people who die from actual physical diseases for deciding to die. Why do we blame those with mental illness?

There are so many of us out there experiencing the same feelings of loss, and asking the same questions. Why did this happen? Why didn't they tell me that they were upset? After a great deal of consideration, I finally decided to share my own unimaginable and horrific tragedy. My hope is that I can help others. I want to share the process of grieving I've gone through so far, what's helped, and what's made things worse. I've experienced thoughts and feelings I thought were not possible to experience. I had no idea these feelings even existed. I've also been surprised by the changes to my relationships with others. I've grown so distant from those I love so much. Probably the worst part of this whole experience has been watching the pain and suffering this suicide has inflicted on my family.

I'm not an expert in psychology or suicide, but I can provide some insight into what it was like to be thoroughly shaken to my core after discovering my son was capable of killing himself. I was the reluctant soldier recruited into a fight I did not believe in, witnessing all the tragedies accompanying it. I can describe how frustrating it is to try to raise a bipolar child, and how difficult it is to handle them. What it is like to struggle for my son's mental well-being harder than he fought for it himself. Even though there was a history of mental illness and a past suicide threat, I was not prepared for the devastating effect of his suicide death. In hindsight, there were many warning signs, and I made so many mistakes. I wish I had a second chance, a chance that was forever stolen from me.

OUR LAST DAY TOGETHER

Stephanie and I wanted to spend a day with the whole family doing something fun together before Christmas. We decided to go out to lunch, go bowling, and then follow up with a holiday movie. Jessie and Joey had the day off from school, and Jeff had the day off also, so it was a perfect opportunity for us to get together. Jeff was reluctant to meet, but Stephanie was quite insistent and he finally relented. She later confessed to me she guilted him into going because nothing else would work. Jeff said he had to take care of some paperwork at the base, so he would miss out on lunch and bowling, but would be available for the film. Jessie was disappointed because Jeff would not be there all day, so she decided to stay home and wrap Christmas gifts. She was getting to the age where being with the family was not cool, and she preferred to have the house to herself. So much for our family day.

We took Joey bowling and then we went out to lunch. During the meal, we started to get texts from Jeff stating he was getting hung up at the base, and he would not be able to join us after all. We went back and forth for a while and finally agreed to attend a later movie so we would not have to cancel.

We arrived at the theatre before Jeff. It was an unseasonably warm day, so we decided to wait outside for him. Joey was running around and playing while Stephanie and I talked on a park bench. We were both frustrated with Jeff because it felt like he was blowing us off and wanted nothing to do with the family. Since he moved out it was becoming increasingly difficult to get him on the telephone, and even more of a challenge to meet face to face. I attributed this behavior to Jeff's desire to be more independent, but Stephanie was sure there was something wrong. She expressed these misgivings to me while we were waiting for Jeff to arrive. I tried to reassure her that this was normal behavior for a twenty-year-old, but she was not convinced. She sensed something was off, she just couldn't put her finger on it. Suddenly Joey ran over to the park bench we were sitting on and said he saw Jeff's car coming. I looked up just in time to see Jeff driving by, and he looked positively furious. I noticed that he was wearing his Navy uniform even though it was his day off. He parked his car and walked toward the movie theatre. He would not look at Stephanie or me directly. Joey ran to him and leaped into his arms. Usually this would put a smile on Jeff's face, but this time was different: the scowl remained. Jeff walked up to me and said nothing. I asked him what was wrong. He replied that he was frustrated with the base because his deployment orders were not ready. He was looking forward to an upcoming training exercise, but he was worried he would be delayed due to the paperwork. I tried to calm him by saying it would not be the end of the world if he was delayed. He did not answer—he just gave me a distant and cold look. Then Jeff did something entirely out of character.

Ever since Jeff had completed Navy basic training, he wore his uniform everywhere he went. He was so proud of being in the military he no longer wanted to wear civilian clothes. Both Stephanie and I had served in the Air Force, but we never wanted to wear the uniform unless it was required. We enjoyed teasing Jeff about this, but he continued to wear the uniform in spite of the jokes. I was surprised when Jeff said, "I need to go to the bathroom and change out of this stupid uniform before we go into the movie." I couldn't believe my own ears: Jeff had never said anything like that before. I stared at him in shock, he said nothing more, and then he walked over to the bathrooms.

We waited for him at the ticket counter while he changed, and then we all went in to the movie together. After the show started, Jeff got up and left. I assumed he was bored with the film because it was a kid's holiday movie. He eventually returned with a soda and popcorn, and did not offer to share with anyone. This was also unusual behavior for Jeff, because he always shared, even when he was a child. Joey asked him for a drink, but Jeff ignored the request. I kept looking at Jeff during the movie, and at one point I thought he was crying. I decided to leave him alone because I knew he would not tell me how he felt even if I asked him directly.

After the movie, we went outside and talked. Joey wanted to see Santa, so we walked over to the attraction and stood in line. While we were waiting to see Santa, I changed my mind and decided to ask Jeff about his deployment again. I assumed this was why he was upset. He told me again how vital it was to him to get to go on the following training deployment because he wanted to get assigned to an active duty unit, and this would not happen if he were delayed. I tried to reassure him things would work out, but he was not convinced.

I can't remember a time in his entire life where he was more upset than he was on that day. I have come to believe Jeff had realized at last that he would never be free of the ties that bound him. He was stuck in a life he hated and, knowing that he couldn't achieve his dreams, he may have felt there was nothing left to live for.

After Joey had finished with Santa, we went back outside to enjoy the fire pit. The sun had set while we were in the movie, and now it was getting cold outside. We warmed our hands by the fire and talked over Christmas plans. Jeff asked me if he could have one of our spare Dyson vacuum cleaners to give to his roommate for a Christmas present. I told him it was too expensive to give away, but he could buy it from me at a discount. I was trying to negotiate with him when Stephanie walked up and told me I should just give him the vacuum. She thought I was being unfair to Jeff. Her comments upset me, so I walked away to calm down.

I ended up on the opposite side of the enormous fire pit from where we had stood during the argument. I looked across the fire and noticed that Jeff had an unusually vacant look in his eyes. He stared back at me with his eyes flat, face impassive. I felt terribly sorry for upsetting him, so I quickly walked back and apologized. His expression remained unchanged, but he said it was all right. I told him he could have the vacuum, but he no longer wanted it. I invited him to come over to watch movies, but he declined. I could feel a sense of panic welling up inside of me. I fell silent, gripped in fear that I couldn't explain. There was something wrong with Jeff, but he was shutting me out, and there was no way I could get him to open up to me.

Jeff finally broke the silence by saying he had to leave. Stephanie and Joey exchanged hugs with Jeff and then it was my turn. I received an exceptionally rigid and stiff embrace. He whispered in my ear, "Goodbye Dad," and then he walked away for the last time.

SUICIDE

December 21, 2011, was just another normal day. I was a software developer, a husband, a father, and I was fairly content with my life. I worked for a company near Denver, and I had been recently promoted. Along with my day job, I had also started my own business writing software for the iPad, and Jeff was my head designer. He was so talented and gifted; I often forgot how young he was because I could talk to him about anything—politics, art, religion. Even though, we had suffered many turbulent years together, I was now naïvely convinced that those growing pains were behind us, and that we had an incredibly exciting future to look forward to.

Since Jeff's completion of Basic Training and A-School, he had been preparing to become a Navy corpsman. I was so immensely proud of him; it was all I talked about with my buddies at work. Jeff's achievements were so much sweeter considering he had almost dropped out of high school and had run away from home before his high school graduation. Although Jeff seemed down at times, his overall demeanor was pretty good. We'd had a bad day yesterday, but I assumed Jeff was just feeling down, and he would be back to normal in no time. I was foolishly confident he was going to be happy and successful.

I had decided to stop by a few stores and do some last-minute Christmas shopping after work, so I called Stephanie at home to let her know I would be a little late. She said it would be okay because she and the other two children were occupied at home, singing Christmas carols and playing the piano.

I finished my shopping and made my way toward the long checkout lines. While I was waiting to pay for the gifts, my cell phone rang. I noticed it was my home number, and I wondered why Stephanie called again since we'd hung up just a few minutes ago. I answered the call and the person on the other end said her name was Linda, and that she was with the Douglas County Sheriff's Department. I thought to myself this must be a prank being played by my older sister Linda, so I went along and said sarcastically, "Yes, Linda, what can I do for you." The voice on the other end of the line said very seriously, "This is Linda with the Douglas County Sheriff's Department. We need you to come home right now, and please drive safely." This answer just did not register in my mind. Why was my older sister at my house, and why was she pretending to be with the Sheriff's Department? Linda repeated herself again, and it finally broke through my confusion: this was not my sister calling me. I began to realize something dreadful had happened. I asked for details, but Linda stonewalled me and reiterated I needed to get home quickly. I said okay, and hung up feeling confused.

My mind was racing, and the police were not telling me anything, so my imagination started running wild. I walked out to my Jeep in the parking lot. A heavy snow was falling, and the wind was blowing like crazy, causing visibility to be next to nothing. I started my Jeep and pulled into the heavy rush-hour traffic. I began to wonder what this could be about. My first thought was that my dad had passed away, and the police wanted to tell me in person. He was seriously ill over the summer from a blood infection, and we had almost lost him. I grabbed my cell phone and called my sister Linda, who had been living with my dad for the past several months. Certainly she could fill me in on the details, and when I knew for sure, it would calm my nerves a little. There was no response on any of her numbers, so I quickly decided to call my other sister, Merri, to see if she knew what the hell was going on. Again, no response. I couldn't believe it. I started to wonder if maybe my sisters were on the telephone with each other and that is why I couldn't reach them. My next call went out to Jeff. I decided if I couldn't get to the bottom of what's going on while I was driving he could start making calls and then fill me in. I got no answer on any of his numbers either, so I decided to call the house again. Besides, I didn't understand why Stephanie didn't call me first, with the police being at the house and all. There was no answer there either, and I was starting to get even more upset. Was this a joke? If so, it was not amusing to me. I had a thirty-minute drive ahead of me, so I decided to stop trying to reach anyone, and try to figure out for myself what was waiting for me when I got home.

I asked myself, why would the sheriff be at my house? Was I in trouble? No, couldn't be—if that were true they probably would have arrested me at work. Besides, I hadn't committed any crimes. Was my dad back in the hospital? Did he pass away? Again I thought to myself it wasn't feasible because one of my sisters would have told me right away. So why were the cops waiting for me at the house? I finally settled on a probable solution.

Jeff was in trouble. He either got into a serious car accident, or he was arrested for something. Jeff was not the most careful driver, so I settled on the idea he was in a traffic accident. I assumed he had been arrested for this accident and the police wanted to accompany me down to county lockup to deal with it. The more I thought about it, the more I was sure this was it. This would also explain why he did not answer his cell phone.

Soon after Jeff got his driver's license he started getting into car accidents all the time. They were mostly fender benders, but it still caused a great deal of grief. When this idea settled into my mind, I remember feeling angry, anxious and fearful. I started to feel angry because now I had to deal with another Jeff problem just before Christmas, but I was also afraid he might be seriously hurt. Of course, these were not new emotions for Stephanie and me. Although Jeff had improved in the last year, I knew he was still capable of getting into trouble.

We live at the edge of a secluded and peaceful state park. Jeff's bipolar was a key factor for this remote choice. We wanted to minimize negative outside influences and be sure we were the main influence in his life. When I pulled into the circular driveway, I saw two unmarked police cars, and the house was ominously dark. During the drive home, I had managed to work myself up into a state of agitation, so I wanted to know what in the hell was going on. I was ready to play bad cop with Jeff to get him to realize his reckless driving affected not only him but the whole family. I pulled into the garage and closed it behind me. I opened the door to the house, and saw a look on Stephanie's face unlike any I had ever seen in 25 years of marriage. She was deadly pale, and her eyes were so swollen, I barely recognized her. Her mouth was moving, but no sound was coming out. One thing I was sure of: this was not a joke, and this may be more severe than a car accident.

I'm not a particularly tall person at five-foot nine inches, and Stephanie is a few inches shorter than me. So when I saw this enormous police officer towering behind her with tears in his eyes too, I started to feel an overwhelming sense of panic. The police officer asked me if I would like to sit down. Unable to control my emotions any longer I shouted "NO, TELL ME WHAT IS HAPPENING RIGHT NOW!" Linda, the other police officer who had phoned me at the store, took my hand, looked me straight in the eye and said the words I will never, ever be able to forget: I'm so sorry, your son Jeff has died.

What did she say? Her words didn't register at first, and then the full effect hit me all at once. I wondered how this could be happening. It seemed surreal to me, and I could feel myself slipping into shock. A nuclear explosion had gone off in my head, and everything was totally obliterated in a single flash. None of this was making any sense to me; this had to be a mistake. Stephanie, Joey and I had spent the previous day with Jeff. We had gone to a holiday movie, and then afterward we had stood outside and talked for a while. Jeff was doing well, and he was extremely excited to come over to the house for Christmas. After the movie Jeff proudly escorted his younger brother Joey to see the shopping mall Santa. Jeff cannot be gone! I started to repeat over and over and over no, no, no, no, no. I knew from that moment on my life would never be the same. I had encouraged Jeff to move out because I wanted to give him space. Why on earth did I allow him to convince me that he no longer needed professional counseling? How could I have been so stupid, naïve and trusting? This is all my fault!

Experiencing this kind of trauma is absolutely nothing like seeing it on TV. I've watched so many violent television shows, death had practically become an everyday occurrence for me. Jeff and I even talked about death sometimes, but of course I assumed it would never really happen in "real life." That's what made the movies fun to watch—they were not real, death was not real. Death is something that happens on the news, to someone else, not to your own children.

When I found out death could visit me personally and take a child from me, all I could do was shed tears of sorrow and pain and scream like a maniac. Even though I knew Jeff was gone, it still didn't seem real to me. It felt like a stupid plot from one of those violent movies I used to watch with Jeff. I couldn't accept this new reality.

In that awful moment, I completely shut down. I couldn't speak, think or stand. I tried to look at Stephanie, through the gusher of tears in my eyes, and repeated, "Jeff is dead?" She shook her head yes, and I started to scream again like I was a twelve-year-old girl at a horror movie. She glared at me and said, "Stop, the kids don't know yet, you have to be quiet." But I couldn't be silent, so I ran into the garage. To this day I don't know what I was planning on doing, but I now know why the massive cop had been dispatched to our house. I was feeling out of control. I wanted to smash and destroy. The police officer solemnly followed me everywhere I went, waiting to intervene. Although I know he had good intentions, he made me feel like I had committed a crime and I was no longer trustworthy. There is no dignity or privacy in suicide.

My emotions rapidly cycled between shock, extreme sadness and anger. I wanted the police to leave, I wanted to be alone, but this was not to be. I paced back and forth in the garage for at least thirty minutes before I was calm and was ready to go back inside the house. Stephanie and Linda were sitting at the kitchen table. When I saw the look on Stephanie's face, I felt another surge of emotion beyond my ability to manage, and began to sob again. The same questions kept popping into my traumatized mind over and over. Why is this happening, how did Jeff die, was it a car accident like I thought?

We all sat down together, and Linda kept looking at Stephanie and then me. I broke the silence and asked, "What happened to Jeff, was it a car accident?" Linda replied, "No, it was a gunshot wound to the head." "Was he murdered?" I asked incredulously. She simply stated that it was a self-inflicted gunshot wound through the mouth, and he died instantly. How could this possibly be? Jeff doesn't have a gun, and besides, I saw him last night, and he was okay. The police began to go over the details.

Jeff was found in his room, lying on his bed. He had positioned pillows around his head, placed the gun in his mouth, and fired, at around two o'clock in the morning. He was extremely intoxicated. His roommates did not hear the gun go off, and he was not discovered until around noon the next day. The police spent the day doing forensics work, and then finally drove out to the house around 6:00 p.m. to deliver the horrible news to us.

Ironically, Jeff had decided to kill himself right when his life was turning around, and he was becoming successful in his Navy career. I couldn't believe he would do such a thing. I thought he was happy, I thought his life was working out for him. I later came to learn that manic-depressives rarely kill themselves while in the depths of depression. They wait to do it until they feel better, are slightly manic, and have the strength to do so. I wondered if this was the case for Jeff. Was he planning this, or was it an impulsive thing for him?

A long painful silence followed and then we were asked if we were ready to tell the children, who had been immediately sent upstairs to watch TV when the police first arrived. We built up our courage and called them down to the kitchen to share the devastating news.

TELLING THE CHILDREN

To me, it felt like we were about to destroy our children's innocence forever, and there was not a damn thing I could do to stop it. All I wanted to do was run away so I would not have to experience what we were about to do. I did not want to have to live with the fact that my son had killed himself. I certainly did not want my kids to live with it either, but in spite of this, we reluctantly called to them. As if we really had a choice.

I could tell the kids knew something was happening, but they were not sure what. Jessie stood beside me, and Joey hopped into Stephanie's lap. Both of them were so concerned for us because we were still crying uncontrollably. Somebody, I don't remember who, ultimately broke the news, and both of them immediately started to cry in unison in a way which was heart-wrenching and devastatingly sad, a sound I will never forget … long, hideous, howling screams of pain as we all sobbed and hugged each other. I felt as if I was going to die from grief right on the spot. I have never seen everyone in my family so upset at the same time. I was convinced we had been irreparably damaged, and we would never be able to recover from this.

My oldest son, my Navy medic, was dead. Stephanie and two children were undoubtedly shattered. Everything I held dear in life felt as if it had been taken away. I held my daughter in my arms and felt her shake wildly. It made me feel completely helpless. My innocent baby girl and beautiful young son were now inextricably caught in the madness that is bipolar disorder and suicide, and I couldn't protect them from it any longer.

JOEY'S REACTION

Jeff's suicide was extremely upsetting to me to say the least, but I was even more concerned about the emotional turmoil Jeff's suicide had produced in my children.

I always knew Joey's young mind was naturally inquiring, and he would not be shy about asking questions, but his first question completely floored me. He wanted to know if he could have Jeff's holiday candy since he was now gone and would not want it. There were many more bizarre questions like that before Joey got around to asking how Jeff had died. We were not comfortable with sharing all the facts with him that night, so we simply said a gun went off accidentally. Stephanie and I knew we should not lie to Joey, but we were not prepared to share the whole truth, at least not yet.

Ultimately it would take nine months to share the actual cause of Jeff's death with Joey. I can honestly say I felt a tremendous sense of relief when we were finally able to tell him the whole truth. On the day we told Joey how Jeff really died, I had attended a suicide survivors' meeting with Jessie, and I had placed the literature on my desk when I got home. Joey noticed the word "suicide" on the papers and asked Stephanie and me what it meant. We had been preparing for this topic, and had decided when he asked we would reveal all the facts about Jeff's death. Our primary goal was to ensure he understood suicide is the result of a disease of the brain, and not to portray Jeff to be an immoral person.

JESSIE'S REACTION

Since Jessie was fifteen at the time Jeff died, we felt she could handle the truth, so she was unlucky enough to bear the full brunt of the story right away. She was much less accepting of Jeff's manner of death than Joey. Her brother had abandoned her, and she was certain that it was all her fault. She spent months wondering if she should have gone to the movies with us the day Jeff took his own life. She felt he would not have killed himself if she had been there for him. She never fully accepted that there was really anything wrong with Jeff. More than anything else, he confided in her, and she in him. Which was why his death was perhaps hardest of all for her. Although I know full well how much the entire family suffered when we lost him, sometimes I feared that Jessie took it the hardest of all. But one cannot measure grief or pain. Who am I to say how deeply the others felt?

TELLING MY FATHER

My father is a sociopath; I've learned this since Jeff's death. I've always wondered how my father was able to recover from the death of loved ones so easily, and now I know the answer. Sociopaths are known to demonstrate the following behaviors.

- Glibness and Superficial Charm

- Manipulative and Conning

- Failure to Recognize the Rights of Others

- Grandiose Sense of Self

- Pathological Lying but Extremely Convincing

- Lack of Remorse, Empathy, Shame or Guilt

- Incapacity for Love

- Constant Need for Stimulation

- Impulsive Nature

- Parasitic Lifestyle

Shortly after the police left the house the day Jeff died, Stephanie called close friends and family. Around 9:00 p.m. I decided to call my father and sister Linda.

They were both on the line when I shared the news of Jeff's death. Linda said she wanted to come over to our home right away to provide emotional support. The reason Linda was living with my father is he had begged her to move in with him about a year before Jeff's death. My father told me Linda needed to share his home because she was broke and required financial aid. I later discovered that he had manipulated Linda and her husband into moving in with him because his second spouse was committed to the hospital with Alzheimer's disease and he was lonely. Linda and her husband were paying for everything.

I had expected my sister to come over, but I was shocked when I saw my dad getting out of her truck in the driveway. After they had come into the house, we all hugged and then sat down together. At the time I did not notice, but my father was the only one not crying. We talked about the details, and Linda offered to help with everything.

Not long after they arrived, my father said he was feeling pain in his back, and wanted Linda to take him home. Before he stepped outside, I asked how he had handled losing his own two-year-old son. He replied by saying, "Don't worry, you will get over it in a few days, life goes on." A few days later I found out he was asking Linda why I was still upset.

During the reception at our home after Jeff's funeral, one of our guests overheard my father glibly say to the Navy liaison, "Well at least there is one person here who gets this isn't the end of the world." In the following months, my father couldn't understand why my mood was so poor, and began to assume I was being hostile toward him. His second spouse died a few weeks after Jeff's funeral. He responded by filling out a profile on an online dating site. He got married again near the one-year anniversary of Jeff's death.

I know I cannot pretend Jeff did not die and that he did not take his own life, the way my father tries to do when dealing with his own losses. I will have to face this pain somehow, and learn to manage it, because if I don't come to terms with the reality that Jeff killed himself, I will never be able to begin mourning him, and I will be exactly like my father: cold, cruel and heartless.

TELLING OTHERS

Shortly after Jeff died, I spent days trying to figure out how I was going to start letting others know what had happened to him, and basically came up with nothing. I couldn't figure out how to pick up the telephone and tell my boss that my son had died by suicide, so I won't be in for a few weeks. How could I call a friend I have not talked to for a while and say, "Hello, I'm calling to let you know my son is dead?" I've heard the phrase "I'm speechless" before, but now I really knew what it meant. In those early weeks I was literally not able to speak. What made this even more difficult was that I had believed Jeff was behaving like an adult and was finally controlling his impulsive behavior—I had no idea how out of control he really was. I felt betrayed and stupid and I did not want anyone to find out the truth.

When I finally built up the courage, I called one of my close friends from work. I hoped I would be able to tell him what happened, invite him to the funeral, hang up, and then call the next person on the list. So I picked up the telephone, dialed, and waited for an answer. When my friend picked up the line and said hello, I found I was unable to say anything. I tried to talk, but the words would not come out. Eventually, I burst into tears and hung up in embarrassment. I spent the next several hours crying. I had lost the ability to communicate with anyone orally. I finally had to resort to using email and texts because speaking was simply impossible for me. I found that even writing a straightforward text or email could take hours to complete.

I'm so thankful I had my sister Linda to help me contact others. She was able to call my office and arrange for a leave of absence, and to call my friends to let them know what was happening. These simple tasks were beyond my capability at the time.

As time wore on, I eventually resumed my ability to communicate with others, although it was extremely difficult at first. Not long after I began speaking about his suicide openly, I had a strong desire to describe what had happened to Jeff to anyone who was willing to listen. It was as if some kind of emotional dam had broken free, and I couldn't stop the flow. I had an insatiable need to talk and share my emotions. I went to lunch with large groups of people and talked about my experience. I attended every group session available and monopolized the conversation. I blogged about his death, I wrote in a journal every day. I even wrote a majority of this book during this time. Strangely, this insatiable need only lasted for a few months, and then I lost the desire to talk about Jeff's suicide at all, even at group therapy sessions. I was becoming increasingly reluctant to share my tragedy with anyone because it was no longer cathartic to share—it was painful. I also felt as if people no longer wanted to hear about it. I didn't know what was happening to me, or why I felt the way I did, but one thing I knew for sure: I needed to complete this book to honor and remember him while I still had the emotional strength to do so.

SEEING YOU AGAIN

Jeff had been dead for several days, but the reality of this horrible news was still not sinking into my brain. He was alive only days ago. It was impossible to absorb or understand, and harder still to believe that he was really gone. I honestly believed there was some mix-up, and he was out of town or something like that. I couldn't let go of the thought that Jeff was still alive; he had to be. I was certain when we showed up to view his body at the funeral home we would find out they had the wrong person. Later we would get a call from Jeff, and he would be all right. I had an overwhelming desire to prove I was right about all of this.

The county coroner was not prepared to release his body to the funeral home, so I called their office and asked them to describe the body they claimed was Jeff. While the coroner talked about his defining features in detail, it slowly began to sink in. This was real. Jeff was gone, there was no mistake. Now I wanted to see Jeff more than ever. I needed to put this fantasy to rest once and for all, and I needed so badly to see him just one more time.

I was worried he would be so disfigured from the gunshot wound we would not be able to lay eyes on him ever again, but about a week after Jeff's suicide we were told we could see him. The funeral home had arranged a private viewing for the family, so we decided to have Merri, my sister from Las Vegas, accompany us to the viewing. Jessie did not want to see Jeff's body, and we did not ask Joey—we made the decision for him not to go. I was worried he would have an unpleasant experience and I wanted to protect him. In retrospect, I wish I had asked Joey, so he could have had the opportunity to decide for himself. Linda volunteered to stay with Joey because Jessie was not in a place to be able to take care of her younger brother.

The funeral home was about an hour away from the house, and I wanted to drive. My sisters and Stephanie all felt it would be too stressful, but I insisted. I needed to feel in control of something, and driving to see my son helped me regain some of it. When we arrived, we were about ten minutes early, so we waited in the parking lot. I was so eager to see him, those last ten minutes felt like ten hours. When our appointed time had arrived, Stephanie and I walked into the lobby and waited for someone to help us. The funeral director walked out and greeted us, and asked if we were ready to see him. We said we were ready, and then we were led into a small chapel where Jeff was placed on a table in front of the room. They had dressed him in a T-shirt and sweatpants because his Navy uniform had not been located yet. I practically ran to the front of the room, I couldn't wait to see him. I just needed to be with him again.

Jeff did not appear to be dead. He looked as if he were sleeping. I stood over his peaceful-looking body and wanted to tell him to "get up, joke's over." I also wanted to reach out and touch him, but at the same time I was afraid of what it would be like. I knew it would be something I would regret if I couldn't be brave enough to do it, so when I gathered enough courage, I gently placed my hands on his shoulder. To my immediate dismay he was extremely hard and cold, but I was not as freaked out as I had thought I would be. I did not leave my hands there for long because it did not seem like Jeff anymore to me. As I examined him closer, I began to see the details that were out of place. His lips were bruised and swollen from the gun, and I could see that his mouth had been sewn shut. The back of his neck was supported by a flexible neck brace because his vertebrae were shattered. His skin had a waxy, cold appearance, and the veins in his hands had collapsed. And it finally started to sink in: he was gone, there is no mix-up, there would be no surprise telephone call. Jeff was truly dead.

I stood there beside his lifeless frozen body and wept for an extremely long time. The release of emotion was so powerful and so painful I started to shake uncontrollably and almost passed out. Stephanie asked if I needed to leave, but this was the last thing I wanted to do. I could have stayed in the room with Jeff forever because I just did not want to say goodbye, ever. I was willing to take whatever I could get even if it was only his cold, broken, dead body; I wanted to be with him. Before seeing my own son this way, I had always wondered why people would obsess over the corpse of a lost loved one. Now I knew firsthand what others felt when they had lost someone so close to them. Besides my memories, pictures and videos, the body was my last tangible physical connection to the boy I had lost. I wanted to take Jeff home with me, and keep him forever. This was not an "empty shell"—this was my precious little boy.

When our time for the viewing had run out, I still couldn't say goodbye. I looked at Jeff and said, "See you later." Leaving him there alone was so difficult, because I knew when we left the funeral home they were going to put him back in the freezer. Stephanie and I walked out to the parking lot and then sat in the Jeep and listened to Fleetwood Mac's "When I See You Again." We cried and held on to each other as the agony of visiting our deceased son washed through us in painful crashing waves.

JEFF'S FUNERAL

When I first had my children, I often imagined myself attending their birthday parties, graduations, and someday their wedding, but on Thursday, December 29, 2011, at 10:00 a.m., Jeff would have his final ceremony, and this was something I never once imagined would be part of our experience together. I now had to accept an unpleasant truth: there would be no more birthday parties, graduations or marriage. I would never get a call at two in the morning saying I was going to be a grandfather. Instead it was a time to say goodbye forever, but I already knew I still would not be able to say it, not now, maybe never. This was going to be the second worst day in my life so far.

We wanted to have a military funeral because of Jeff's service in the Navy, but we were unsure if this would be possible since Jeff had killed himself. The funeral home contacted the Navy liaison for us, and to our relief they agreed to participate. This meant there would be a large Navy presence at the chapel, a twenty-one gun salute at the gravesite, and at the conclusion of the service we would be presented with the American flag that would cover his coffin during the service. Most of the guests would not realize Jeff had died by suicide;

rather they would think he died while serving his country. Only close friends and relatives would know the truth.

Along with the military honors we decided to make a memorial video for Jeff, highlighting his life with photos and music. We chose images spanning his entire life, including birthday parties, graduation ceremonies and trips to the playground. We concluded the slide show with one of the last photos I had taken of Jeff when he was actively accepting treatment and before bipolar began ravaging his mind. The photo was taken on the edge of a cliff right as the sun was beginning to disappear behind the mountains. Jeff was awash in golden rays of light, and he was happy, and at peace. We were all happy. At the time I took his picture I thought the sunset was especially beautiful, so I decided to take two shots, one with Jeff in the frame and one with only the setting sun. Before Jeff died, the sunset picture without him in it was one of my favorites because the light at the center was in the shape of a heart. Now that he is gone the photo has become a symbol of my loss and suffering because he is missing from the frame and my life. Now the light only reminds me of how my soul is broken and how much I miss him.

Hundreds of people came to pay their last respects. We had a minister deliver Jeff's eulogy, and then we played our video. After the video was over, people were invited to share their thoughts and condolences. Stephanie and I were unable to speak, but Joey and Jessie did come up and share their thoughts. My heart ached seeing them stand in front of the room, sobbing while they shared memories of their brother. I couldn't believe the strength of character they both displayed. Although it made me intensely sad, I was so very proud of them. At the conclusion of the ceremony, members from Jeff's Naval unit recited the Corpsman's Oath in his honor. Then the most difficult part was about to begin— the receiving line and the final viewing. Stephanie, the kids and I were seated in the front row near the exit. The minister announced there would be a viewing, and all were welcome to stay if they wished; otherwise they may offer condolences to our family and leave the chapel.

Greeting each person was incredibly painful. I was like a robot, shaking hands and thanking them for coming. In reality, I was going crazy and hanging on for dear life. It was a blur of faces and sounds and agonizing memories, intense pain, and constant tears. I wanted to run away, and never come back. The greeting was optional; why on earth did I agree to do it.

When all the people that did not want to see Jeff's body had left the chapel, Jeff's coffin was reopened. I found I had the same response; I wanted to spend the rest of the day with him. I did not want the coffin closed. Jeff was dressed in his Navy whites, the same uniform he returned home in after completing Navy A-School. The uniform was absolutely perfect, like it was when he was alive. I did not want to touch him this time because of how he had felt a few days before: cold and lifeless. All I could do was stare at him in his casket and weep.

Seeing him there reminded me of when he was a baby lying in his bassinet asleep. He was dressed all in white then too, resting peacefully, waiting for his life to unfold. Now that life was over; there would be no new adventures for him. He would spend the rest of eternity in this box. Others came forward to see him and then left, but I never left his side. Eventually, the time had come to seal his casket forever. I watched the men slowly close the lid on him and thought to myself: this is it, he is gone, and I will never get him back, I will never see him again. His coffin was then loaded onto the hearse, and we started the funeral procession to the gravesite.

At Jeff's grave, words were spoken which I can no longer remember, the Navy delivered the twenty-one gun salute, and his coffin was lowered into the ground. We dropped flowers into his grave, and then it was over. Jeff was now officially dead and buried, but the family's pain and suffering was only beginning.

PRIOR LOSS

Recovering from a major loss is like being forced through a twisting maze that presents you with one dead end after another. To complete the journey successfully requires perseverance more than anything else.

I have suffered many losses in my lifetime that I felt were disheartening and unbearable. However none of these previous experiences even came close to the level of misery and suffering losing a child to suicide brings. Suicide leaves the lives of those left behind shattered into millions of tiny pieces, and we simply don't know how to start cleaning up the catastrophic damage. Contending with any death is difficult, but suicide intensifies the agony because we are forced to deal with two traumatic situations at the same time. Before Jeff's death, I accepted that life had ups and downs, and I had to deal with them; but Jeff's suicide has affected me in ways I struggle to understand. In a small way, I feel deceived. Jeff should have been able to share how he was feeling with me. I thought we were remarkably close. He knew how much I cared about him and yet he treated me like a stranger. Before I experienced suicide, I believed it did not exist. It seemed so remote and unreal until it happened to someone I loved.

When I was three years old I had a brother; his name was also Jeffrey. He was one year younger than me. At the time, both Jeffrey and I were extremely sick with pneumonia. My mother had taken us to the doctor that day, and by the time she got us home she was physically and emotionally drained. She asked my father to stay up and keep checking on us through the night. I truly believe he meant to do what she asked, but instead he fell asleep on the couch and failed to check on us. My dad could fall asleep on the couch in the middle of a hurricane. To our family's horror, my younger brother Jeffrey passed away in the room we shared during the night that my father was supposed to keep watch. I was far too young to remember what happened when Jeffrey's body was discovered in the morning, but I can imagine it was not good. By the time I was old enough to ask about Jeffrey, my questions were always dismissed with short answers stating Jeffrey is in heaven now, and he is clearly in a better place. I was unaware at the time, but this was a profound loss, and beneath the surface I was suffering terribly. The adults in my life were not willing or able to talk about it with me.

When I was around eleven years old, my grandmother moved into the family's basement because she was disabled and unable to care for herself. During her stay with us, she and I became extremely close. I had spent countless hours listening to her stories, and telling her about my own adventures. She was a captive audience and seemed to have infinite patience for me. This was something I couldn't get from my parents because they were always "busy."

Her husband, my grandfather, had died just before I had been born and she missed him terribly. She was also suffering from severe arthritis. The disease had stolen the use of her legs and grotesquely twisted her fingers and toes. Her pain was quite intense, and sometimes when her mood was dark or her pain felt intolerable, she would tell me she wished that she could die, so she could join her husband in heaven to escape her tortured existence. I did not understand how she could say such horrible things, and would immediately disagree with her, stating emphatically that she couldn't die, because I loved her too much for that to happen. She eventually proved my statement to be utterly false.

One spring morning I was getting ready to go down and say good morning to her before school. My father stopped me in the hallway. He said, with a smile on his face, that Grandma had died peacefully in her sleep and was now in heaven with Grandpa and my brother Jeffrey. My father seemed to be perfectly happy for her, and suggested I should be happy for her too. I was then sent to school like any other ordinary day.

I was absolutely shocked and was certainly not happy for her, or me. This was an unacceptable tragedy, and I couldn't understand how this could be happening. Her funeral was held in our church, and it was an open-casket ceremony, for which I was not prepared. When I approached the casket and touched her, she was cold and hard, and I freaked out. I was removed from the church, and was not allowed to attend the rest of the funeral, or the burial. Although it took several years, I eventually stopped dreaming about my dead grandmother. Attempts to talk about how I felt were quickly dismissed with the usual reply, "She is in a better place now, you should be happy for her." My pain would not be acknowledged by the adults in my life, especially my father, so I would have to sort out the pieces for myself much later.

Many years later, after I was married and had two children of my own, my mother inexplicably collapsed when she was cleaning her shower. My father rushed her to the emergency room, where she then fell into a coma. He called me a few days after the incident, and told me not to worry, but my mother has been in a coma, and he thought I should know. Over the years, my father had become so disconnected that even the possibility of his wife unexpectedly dying did not seem to bother him in any way. I was intensely angry with him for taking so long to inform me of my mother's illness, and I told him so. He simply said he did not want me to worry. My mother eventually came out of the coma, but she never truly recovered.

Within a few short years, I found myself standing at the foot of her deathbed at the hospice, literally waiting for her to stop breathing. The whole family was gathered around, all trying to comfort her in her last moments, except for me—I was downright speechless. When she finally drew her last breath, I can remember having the same feeling I'd had when I found out my grandmother had died years before: total confusion and shock. Even though I'd known this day was coming and I had prepared for it, I still had an extremely difficult time accepting she was gone. My father, in classic form, waited about a minute and then announced, well this body is an empty shell now, and your real mother is in heaven. He then walked out of the room as if nothing had happened, followed by the rest of the family except me. I was frozen in place, still not able to believe what I had witnessed. Many years later, this moment, and its callous handling by my father, still has the power to upset and anger me. I've not been able to forgive him for his selfish and uncaring attitude.

Although my mother was now gone, the worst part of the drama was yet to come. My father is not a patient person, to say the least. My mother had stated in her will that she would like to be cremated, and have her ashes spread across one of her favorite lakes in the Colorado Rockies. She was cremated shortly after her death, but schedules and weather were not cooperating with the spreading of the ashes, and several months had passed. Finally, my father became so impatient he demanded we all meet on the following weekend and fulfill my mother's last wishes no matter what. My oldest sister Linda had a boat, so she was asked to bring it along so we could ride out to the center of the lake together, pay our last respects, and then spread her ashes.

On the appointed day, Linda was the last of us to arrive at the lake. She looked positively exasperated:

although she had brought the boat, she informed us all she couldn't get it to start. My father became angry, walked toward the lake with my mother's ashes in his hands and said, "I'll just have to do this myself." Without regard for anyone else in the funeral party, he marched toward the shore. In a state of shock, we began to follow. He waded two feet past the edge of the water line, ripped the lid off of my mother's urn and dumped her remains into the water as if they were garbage. There was a breeze blowing, and he was upwind from us. My mother was no longer in heaven; a good portion of her was on us and in my son Jeff's mouth. Before this experience, I did not realize there are bone fragments in the ashes.

Jeff was eight years old at the time, and my daughter Jessie was two. My mother had been ill for several years before she died, so there had been a great deal of stress related to her long illness, but this incident took the cake. I was angry and I fell into a deep depression in the following months, but I was able to continue working. At this point in my life, I thought I had been dealt about the worst cards a person could be dealt. My mother was recently deceased, and I had lived out a scene from *The Big Lebowski*.

SPECIAL DAYS

The first few years after losing Jeff to suicide were nearly unbearable. Every day seemed to be more difficult than the day before it, but wedding anniversaries, holidays and birthdays were the worst days of all. Holidays can be tough times to begin with, but they are particularly difficult for parents who have lost children to suicide. These days only serve as reminders that you are in pain; they do not feel like times to celebrate. They remind you that you have lost someone very significant to you. They highlight the emptiness you feel inside.

The emotions I felt on these days were often as strong as, or even more powerful than, how I felt when Jeff first died. What makes matters worse is friends and relatives still want to celebrate these days together, even though you do not. I had to exclude myself from all holiday activities because they were just too overwhelming, and I always felt as though I was dampening everyone's spirits because I was still so depressed.

The first holiday we had to deal with after Jeff died was Christmas, and there was no way to avoid it. Joey still believed in Santa Claus and the house was completely decked out for the Yuletide celebration to come. There were piles of gifts under the tree and tons of food in the fridge. We had spent weeks getting ready. Just a few days before Jeff died, he came over to the house and helped decorate the Christmas tree. Our tree was a focal point of the holiday tradition because we had been collecting Hallmark ornaments for over 25 years, and they held a highly significant meaning to the family. We bought ornaments for each member of the family every year and after two and a half decades we had amassed a huge collection. Each ornament seemed to have its own story to tell, its own special set of memories from past Christmases.

This year, since Jeff was now living on his own, we decided to give him our first Christmas tree, and all the ornaments we had been collecting for him since he was born. Although he seemed unmoved by the gesture, my wife and I felt confident the sentimentality of the gift would sink in eventually. Our new family tree was twelve feet tall and entirely covered with the rest of the ornaments. Jeff had the honor of hanging all the "high" ones this year since he was now an adult.

Looking at the tree after Jeff died on that first Christmas morning was beyond painful. We considered canceling, but since Joey was still excited to celebrate, we did not want to upset him even more than he already was, so we carried on with the usual holiday traditions anyway. Opening gifts, cooking dinner, and watching holiday movies was an absolute nightmare. I couldn't wait for that awful day to be over. After a few weeks, I started to take down the tree, and put the other decorations away. I wanted to remove the horrible reminders of Jeff's holiday suicide, because every decoration, every ornament now evoked massive waves of pain and emotional distress. I put everything in the storage room, and I have not been able to bring it out since the Christmas we lost Jeff.

My worst decision for that holiday season was my choice of gifts for Jeff. I knew he loved to drink coffee, so I wanted to get him a personalized coffee mug. After an exhaustive search, I finally settled on what I thought would be the perfect choice, a black coffee mug with a gun shaped pistol grip. I thought this would be a clever present because we had argued over guns for so many years. I had no idea Jeff had a real gun, and I certainly did not know what he was about to do with it. The irony of this gift choice still continues to haunt me.

Christmas was not the only holiday we had to figure out how to get through. Besides the usual holidays, we had Stephanie's birthday in January, Joey's in February, and our wedding anniversary in April. Along with everything else we were trying to deal with, Stephanie's estranged parents both died within a month of Jeff's funeral, and so did my stepmother. Stephanie was so totally overwhelmed by all of it that she started to have a nervous breakdown, a breakdown I was not able to handle. I persuaded her to fly back east and visit with friends for a few months so we could calm down and she could tend to some family affairs back home. This meant she would miss Joey's birthday, something she would never do under normal circumstances. I barely endured Joey's ninth birthday without her. Having her miss the party was such a traumatic experience for me; I became ill and spent the next week in bed having my own breakdown.

Stephanie returned from her trip shortly before spring break. My sister Merri offered to have us come visit her in Las Vegas, and we accepted. She made the week as enjoyable as any person could have, but in spite of her tremendous efforts it couldn't penetrate through the pain we were suffering at the moment.

We painfully endured the rest of the year's holidays and found ourselves facing Jeff's birthday in October. Normally I love October because of the weather and the changing colors, but this year I felt different for obvious reasons. We tried to make his birthday special by taking the day off as a family to commemorate his memory. We went to the movies and out to lunch. Afterward we bought balloons and released them at Jeff's grave. The anticipation of the day was much worse than the day itself, but it was still extraordinarily difficult.

When Christmas came around for the second time, we decided to go to Disneyland. The break helped, but the emotions were still remarkably strong.

Special Days continue to cause emotional distress, but the intensity has lessened over time. I wonder if I will ever enjoy any of them ever again.

ALONE

"Sorrow comes in great waves ... but it rolls over us, and though it may almost smother us, it leaves us on the spot and we know that if it is strong, we are stronger, inasmuch as it passes and we remain."

—Henry James

Since Jeff ended his own life, I've never felt so totally isolated and detached from the rest of the world. I was in no way prepared for the violent extremes of emotion that would envelop me after his suicide. Even when surrounded by my friends and my family I felt alone because I was fully engulfed in a self-imposed prison of anger, guilt and despair. In most cases, I could feel myself physically shrinking away when I would come across others because I no longer felt that I belonged. Jeff was dead, I was living, and I felt a pain and suffering that would never end. I repeatedly asked myself how I was going to get through the rest of my life without my beloved son. I couldn't be distracted from the horror of what he had done to himself, to his life, and to the lives of those who loved him so dearly. How could this terrible, seemingly pointless act of self-inflicted violence have occurred in my family? I wondered how it was it possible that his desperate state of mind had gone unrecognized and untended. I should have known what he was planning, I should have been able to anticipate and prevent his death. I found little comfort in my family, my grieving spouse and my two bereaved children, who shared the agony of this tragedy. My family was permanently broken because one of us would be missing forever. I was inconsolable, and I believed my life was over. Although I never doubted my life would continue, I saw its continuance only as pain-filled days, stretching endlessly into years to be endured without peace of mind or any promise of happiness.

For months, I remained trapped, isolated, and powerless. I was obsessed with my son's suicide, with finding the cause; it was the first and last thought of every day. My every heartbeat underscored his death and my loss; every moment was consumed by sadness and misery. I was exhausted by the endless waves of negative emotions.

Most people had no idea of the level of hell I was going through because I was always faking happiness or well-being to avoid the painful subject of his death. The absolute agony of accepting his suicide has been the most overwhelming and crushing experience I've ever had to confront, and others simply couldn't comprehend how difficult it was for me to handle, regardless of how hard I tried to explain what I was feeling. Besides, I was not capable of explaining the complexity of emotions I was experiencing anyway, so I usually avoided the subject. I forced myself to go through the motions of living, performing routine daily tasks. I tried to give comfort to my family, but it was only a thin façade, a shallow veneer around a massive cold nothingness. I was consumed with self-loathing and tormented by the idea that something I had done or had failed to do may have robbed my son of his desire to live. I thought I would explode from the embroiling force of rage, guilt and frustrated helplessness. Many times I struggled with a certain mood and found relief from having "finished" with that part of the great complexity of my emotions, only to have it happen again, confusing and nagging in its persistence to be reprocessed. Everywhere I went, every conversation I had, I felt the "elephant in the room." I always worried that the person I was talking to would ask me how I was doing. I would argue with myself whether I wanted to answer the question honestly, or say I was doing okay, because Jeff's absence was the only thing on my mind. When I did risk speaking of his suicide, people's well-intentioned advice and words of comfort often came across as ignorant and sometimes felt cruel. Although they tried to relate to my grief with comments like, "I cannot imagine what you must be going through" it only increased the feeling of seclusion even more because their lives were still normal.

Some people would pretend that they didn't hear me, or act as if I just told them the weather is going to change. They were incapable of any compassion or understanding. It is because of these people and their responses that I decided it was too risky to share my feelings any longer. The awkwardness I felt in these situations was beyond measure. I ultimately decided I would not talk about Jeff unless I was in a very safe environment. It is a fact: unless you have experienced this type of loss yourself, you simply will not be able to understand how it feels to lose a child to suicide. I envied people who had the luxury to concern themselves with such minor annoyances as a spot ruining their shirt or being delayed in a traffic jam. The roller coaster of emotions I felt following his suicide caused such strong feelings of isolation, I couldn't connect with people as I used to. I struggled with the challenge of putting the pieces of my life back together. I needed to find a way to reestablish my identity. It seemed as if I were on a never-ending spiral downward with any chance of hope being only a faint dream and happiness an absolute impossibility. There were so many more agonizing days than happy. I would try so hard to engage, but the horror inside my brain overrode everything else. My sister Linda is fond of saying, "fake it till you make it." I have the "fake it" part down pat, but I am most certainly not doing exceptionally well with the "make it" piece.

While some people were comforting and understanding, many more unreservedly rejected my family. We quickly learned that facing the stigma of suicide is extremely painful, because people were sorry for us when they first learned Jeff had died, but then they backed off when they heard the word suicide. If his cause of death were something accidental, I bet these people would have been much more sympathetic and understanding. Many want nothing to do with those associated with the suicide victims, and recoil at the subject. People we thought were close friends ignored us, making it look like the family would be in solitude forever. We were closed off from the encouraging words mourners commonly heard, and instead suffered the deafening sound of silence. It is as if we had somehow brought the situation on ourselves, so we should not expect any sympathy from others. At times, it seemed impossible to maintain a sense of hope, peace and dignity while we worked through the long, and painful, healing process.

My obsession with his death not only made everyday situations difficult to manage. I couldn't sleep, eat, concentrate, work or relax. I only focused on how much I missed him, and how incredibly angry I was that he took his own life. Jeff never said goodbye. He never let on that he was contemplating killing himself. There was no note, no clue as to what had gone wrong. I wanted him back, I wanted my old life back, and I wanted to feel like me again.

The cost suicide exacts on survivors is extremely high. Although I began to realize that Jeff most likely completed suicide in a desperate attempt to end his own pain, his deep distress had not been extinguished; rather, it just passed on to the rest of the family. In the wake of a loved one's death by suicide, families often deteriorate, unable to deal with the intense grief and the complex, painful, and often unanswerable question of "Why?" Beyond grief and the fruitless search for answers, survivors of suicide also grapple with crippling emotions. The endless waves of emotions that run through the minds of suicide survivors can be so overwhelming that they cause the person to no longer be able to function. Life just seems to stop for them, now that their loved one has died by suicide.

Stephanie was suffering from a debilitating depression, Joey was angry all of the time, and Jessica was totally withdrawn. I was furious with Jeff because this selfish act had created more pain and sorrow in the family, not stopped it. His suicide destroyed the original fabric of the family and exacerbated all the problems that already existed, causing them to grow deeper and more entrenched. People are inclined to think everyone will rally together at a time of loss, but that turns out to be more fantasy than fact. Sometimes, relationships can be damaged for years. Sometimes they are permanently destroyed. In either case, the sadness of the loss is multiplied many times over. After Jeff died, I became an unwilling participant in all family events because I was so overwhelmed with guilt, pain and sorrow. Every holiday, birthday, or festive occasion was now torture to me. I was missing out on everything wonderful, and I feared this would be a permanent change.

The suicide of a child can also contribute to the destruction of a marriage. Current statistics show there is a seventy percent divorce rate among surviving couples of child suicides. Stephanie's character was so tied to being Jeff's mother that after his death, she only had a faint connection to the rest of the family and life itself. His death was not a shared loss; it was a personal loss for each of us to manage on our own. Even though we talked about his death often, our personal pain divided us, and any intimacy we once shared was all but destroyed because we were too engulfed by guilt and grief to feel anything else. We isolated ourselves from each other because we were both afraid of hurting one another more than we already were.

There are two significant hurdles to overcome when dealing with a suicide. First, we have to come to terms with the fact that the beloved was capable of taking their own life; and then we have to mourn their loss. In a desperate attempt to understand the reasons behind the unexpected and sudden suicide of my son, I've read numerous books, blogs and pamphlets related to the subject. I've been to counseling and attended several group therapy sessions. I've discovered others feel the same things I'm feeling, and although this has not made the pain of my loss subside, I now know I am not alone. There is solace in knowing others have somehow survived this unbearable tragedy, and maybe I will also. For those of us who have survived the suicide of a loved one, life will never be the same again; the suicide has fundamentally changed us and totally redefined our relationships with others.

IT IS MY FAULT

When a child deliberately ends their life, grief is intensely compounded. Because I am a father, I also have tremendous potential for feeling guilt. While I may be able to forgive myself for being unable to intervene at the moment of Jeff's suicide, I found myself constantly dwelling on all the mistakes I made in raising him. I endlessly reconstruct his death in my mind; I dwell on the moments leading up to his suicide, moments when, I think, I should have been able to prevent his death by doing or saying the right things at the right times. Guilt has a way of permeating every aspect of the grieving process, but I know to heal I must find a way to distinguish Jeff from his suicide. "Where did I go wrong?" "Did I push him too hard?" "If only I had been more patient and understanding." These questions are but a few of the items on my list of self-allegations. I try to remind myself that, while I had considerable influence over Jeff's life, I did not personally create every aspect of it. From his earliest years, he was shaped by an assortment of outside influences beyond my control. Friends, school, movies, music videos, games and the world at large played key roles in shaping his personality. Additionally, I realize Jeff has to take responsibility for his actions. Jeff had the ability to complete suicide; therefore, he was responsible for the suicide. I especially did not have control of his mental illness since he was an adult and refused treatment of any kind.

Although I continue to struggle with guilt for Jeff's death, I have gradually come to believe no person, even a father, is the sole influence on another's life. I have discovered in group sessions that guilt is one emotion that seems to be universal to all survivors of suicide, and overcoming it is one of the most difficult obstacles on the path to healing. Guilt is your worst enemy because it is a false accusation. I repeat over and over in my mind: I'm not responsible for Jeff's suicide in any way, shape, or form. I write it down repeatedly, even when it seems artificial, because I know deep in within my soul it is the truth. I must find a way to forgive both of us for his self-inflicted death.

I often ask myself why so many suicide survivors tend to blame themselves. Many psychiatrists theorize that human nature subconsciously resists so strongly the idea we cannot control all the events of our lives that we fault ourselves for a tragic event rather than accept our inability to stop it. One of the most remarkable aspects of survivor guilt is that it is usually a solo trip because each survivor tends to blame primarily themselves. I began asking others who were also mourning Jeff about any guilt feelings haunting them. In most cases, I found each person, no matter how close or removed they were from Jeff, willingly took the majority of the blame on themselves. If they were the one closest to him, they theorized, "I should have known exactly what was going on in his mind." If they were distanced from him, they often said, "If I'd only been closer to him…" Since we cannot all be to blame, who was responsible for his suicide? I began to wonder if it was possible that none of us was to blame, and if that were true, who should be held responsible for Jeff's suicide? The truth of the matter is only one person is responsible for any suicide: the victim. That is a tough pill to swallow, so instead of ascribing blame to Jeff, we all nobly took responsibility on ourselves.

I have also learned that the guilt I feel is anger turned inward. His suicide created many painful and confusing emotions for me, but one of the strongest emotions I experienced was frustration. Frustration at being so violently cut off from him and the opportunity to help him. This frustration produced anger, and when I turned this outrage upon myself it became guilt. Another source of my guilt came from an unfounded assumption that others were silently blaming me for his death. Since I am a parent, I feared the world at large would label me as a failure because of my son's suicide. While some ignorant people may think or even speak such accusations, most did not, so I needed to avoid projecting negative thoughts onto others by judging myself for them.

I have often found myself feeling guilty when I find myself laughing, having a good time or simply enjoying life since his suicide. Although there is no set timetable for grieving, I realize that if a significant time passes and I am still not allowing myself to move on, instead allowing myself to be crippled with guilt for something that was not my fault… I need to ask myself why.

In any situation, most people don't engage in behavior they don't receive a reward for. Is the fact that I cannot heal a reward? If I believe the only link I have with Jeff is my grieving, could that be a reward? Is the guilt a reward? Am I punishing myself because I think I deserve to be punished for being a worthless person because I allowed him to die? If I want to forgive myself, I have to understand that guilt is all about intention. Was there a single bone in my body that wished that something terrible would happen to Jeff? If not, then why do I feel guilty?

Feeling such love and empathy toward Jeff makes it understandable that I was reluctant to place blame on him. The key lies in understanding the difference between accountability and responsibility. Blame is accusatory and judgmental, but assigning responsibility need only be a frank acknowledgement of the fact. Suicide victims may not have much control over their actions if clinical depression is at the root. If this is true, then I could easily see Jeff's suicide as a disease. His illness killed him as surely as if it had been cancer. This could explain why Jeff may not deserve blame for his suicide. However, on some level, he had made a conscious choice. So the responsibility ultimately lies with him. Acknowledging this fundamental fact doesn't mean I did not love him, nor does it mean I am holding him in contempt, it means I am looking at this tragic event clearly, and accepting it for what it is.

Handling a suicide loss is a deeply personal experience. Although there were others to help support me through the process, no one could help me go through it more easily or understand all the emotions I was going through. The best thing I could do is to feel the pain, because resisting it only prolongs the natural healing process. Many polls and studies have revealed it takes most people at least two years to begin returning to a normal life after a significant loss. There is even danger in establishing two years as a reasonable goal. The truth is it's finished when it's finished. Very little is reasonable about grief. There is nothing sensible, rational, or fair about losing someone we love. There is nothing rational about any major loss. Whatever the loss, the experience is devastating. The last thing any of us needs at such a time is to feel guilty because we aren't responding in the "right" way. Grief is the last act of love we have to give those who have died.

At some point, there will come a time when I may feel that enough is enough and I no longer need to experience the pain. When this time arrives I will need to remind myself that giving up the pain will not cause me to lose my memories of Jeff. How long I grieve or how strongly I hurt doesn't indicate how much I loved him. The fact that it has been three, five or ten years and I am allowing myself to live life doesn't mean I love Jeff any less, and it certainly doesn't mean I've forgotten him either. When I am willing to let go of my guilt and grief,

I will talk out loud to him, expressing my continued love while affirming my decision to let go. I may feel guilty about feeling good. I'll laugh at a joke, smile at a movie, or enjoy a breath of fresh, spring air, and then it will hit me: "How dare I feel good?" I need to understand that feeling guilt when positive emotions start resurfacing is not uncommon, because it feels as if I'm minimizing his death. I will try to avoid feeling guilty for enjoying the natural pleasures in life because I am entitled to them as much as anyone, if not more. There will be plenty of time for tears; I want to take whatever happiness life sends my way, no matter how small or temporary.

GRIEVING

The one experience that binds all human beings together is experiencing a significant loss. A major loss is any loss experience that destroys a significant piece of what makes our lives normal. It might be the death of a loved one, a catastrophic injury to oneself, a traumatic divorce, or relocation to another city. These major losses happen to everyone without regard to economic status, ethnic origin, religious belief, or gender. If there is any good news, it is that we are never the only one to feel as we do. No one can begin to describe the incredible depth of pain we feel when a loved one dies. If you have already had that experience, you understand. The emotional pain is beyond words. Therefore, no response is more normal or appropriate than grief. The hardest time to learn about the grieving process is while you are in the midst of it. Learning how to grieve effectively is the most important skill anyone can learn. You may think you are taking a crash course in grief and that the learning curve is daunting, but those who seek to understand grief and death will be better equipped to recover. Grief affects everything you do, and it can disrupt every aspect of your life in ways you might not expect. One reason for this is that your loss is not just one solitary loss; it is many losses all at once. You will miss so many qualities and facets of the person who died that each will become an opportunity to experience grief. The variety of things you need to grieve may surprise you. Recovering from a major loss is not like getting over the flu. Grief is not an illness. It doesn't help to take two aspirin, go to bed, and wait for the grief to go away. Neither is there enough alcohol in the world to make the pain disappear. When you experience a major loss, it is as though the rug of life has been jerked out from under you. Someone or something that gave life meaning and joy for you is gone forever. You don't know which way to turn or what to do. Getting back on your feet is a difficult but important first move toward recovery. It can take much longer than you expect to feel normal again.

The loss of a loved one is a profoundly painful experience, but the grief experience is not the same for everyone. Everyone who loves is vulnerable to the pain of grief. Love means attachment, and all attachments are subject to loss. Grief doesn't need to be a destructive emotion. Grief is not an enemy or a sign of weakness. Grief is the cost of loving someone. Unfortunately, the death of a loved one is something everyone will experience at some point in his or her life, and modern American culture does little to prepare us for it. We need only look at the emphasis on staying young and healthy in the hope of living forever to realize we live in a culture that prefers to not recognize the existence of death and disease. You can get through every major loss without being destroyed by it. You can enjoy life to the fullest, knowing all the while that it will end. Everybody is capable of becoming good at doing grief work.

Healthy grief is not a passive experience. It isn't something that happens to you. The loss is what happens to you; grief is the normal, appropriate response to loss. Grieving is what you do to heal the wounds in your life after a significant loss. There is much more for you to do in response to any loss than just wait and suffer. You can take charge of your own grief process. You are the one who can turn the pain of any loss into a creative hurt; an experience from which you learn and grow.

Since grief is personal and is something that you do, the one who is in charge of it is you. Taking charge of your own grief is something you can do, but there will be many times when you really don't want to. Taking charge of your grief means doing some specific things, including: Making the conscious choice that you will live. Giving yourself permission to have a life that doesn't include the one who has died, except in memory. Putting yourself in a grief support group. Facing and accepting the myriad of feelings that flood over you. Taking care of your physical needs. Allowing others into your personal life. Over the course of time, becoming willing to invest your love and emotions in other people, while recognizing they could be taken from you. Finding simple ways to take time out from grieving.

The loss of an immediate family member to suicide creates an added depth and complexity to your grief, because you shared a memorable and intimate connection. This relationship helped define who you are as a person. Losing them rips you apart inside, leaving you unsure of your own identity.

While I struggle with the delicate balance between going forward and not forgetting about Jeff, I found the pain did ease slightly over time. I had to be honest about my relationship with him, because I sometimes caught myself reinventing the relationship we really had, sometimes making it better, sometimes making it worse, than it probably was. I worked on remembering the good as well as the bad. I slowly began to put my life back together, and I slowly found the impossible rawness of my pain was replaced by a dull ache of remorse for his uncompleted life. When I began to move on, I discovered that I still had the capacity to laugh and love, and even to be concerned about everyday worries of the everyday world around me. Gradually there were minutes, then hours, and then longer periods of time when suicide was not the focus of my life.

Assess your state of health before your loss. If you have been under a doctor's care recently, or if you have a history of heart problems, stroke, high blood pressure, or any other serious health problem, get in touch with your doctor at once.

Be cautious about what you eat and drink. Food may not interest you at all. Nonetheless, you need all the energy and emotional strength you can gather. Going long periods of time without eating, then consuming foods with little or no nutritional value, or drinking large quantities of beverages with caffeine or alcohol, is not helpful.

Talk about the deceased person. Talk with anyone and everyone who will listen to you. Think back about past good times and tell stories that are unique to the one who has died. Don't hesitate to talk about the events surrounding the death. You may find yourself telling the story of how the death occurred over and over. That's normal and good.

Make time for solitude. Don't be afraid of your emotions. Not even hysteria will hurt you.

Keep your routine intact as much as possible. Go to bed as close to your normal bedtime as possible, even if you don't feel like sleeping. Avoid tranquilizing yourself with medication, drugs, or alcohol.

The following information guided me as I worked my way through the slow and painful grieving process.

What I Experienced Physically

- Lack of desire to eat or sometimes a desire to overeat

- Inability to sleep

- Headaches

- Stomach disorders

- Tightness in the throat or in the muscles

- Heaviness or pressure in the chest

- Visual or auditory hallucinations of Jeff

- Low energy levels

- Periods of anxiety or even panic

What I Experienced Emotionally

- Overwhelmed with emotion

- Sadness and depression

- Mood swings

- Cry easily and unexpectedly

- Forgetfulness

- Inability to concentrate

- Difficulty making decisions

- Guilt

- Anger toward others and Jeff

- Desire to run away or get active to avoid pain

- Feelings of discomfort around other people

- Feelings of emptiness

- Doubts or questions concerning why the death occurred

- Fear of what would happen next

Although the grief of suicide is more difficult to deal with than loss from a disease or other natural cause, gradually, in my own experience, I began to get some solace with his death. Here are some other things to keep in mind while grieving a suicide.

- Those who have lost a loved one due to natural causes may not understand all the complexities of a loss from a suicide.

- Suicide has its own deeper level of denial and shock. The event is unbelievable, unexpected, and tragic all at once.

- You may feel anger longer and deeper than from other deaths. Find constructive ways to let your anger out, give yourself permission to be angry.

- Look for forgiveness in your time, not others'. Forgiveness comes from within, not from a "should forgive" place. When friends tell you the stories of how a victim's family found peace, know they are in pain because they see you in pain.

- The trauma of losing someone to suicide takes hold quickly and leaves family members totally bewildered.

Emotions can be tremendously overwhelming when we are grieving, so much so that getting through the day can feel like an impossible task. There are no fixed guidelines for the recovery process: we each heal in our own time and in our own way. Our suffering is as unique as the lives of those we have lost. Any major loss is a personal experience. Your loss is yours, regardless of how many other people are affected by it. Because of this, it will be difficult to share your feelings with others. It will be equally difficult for anyone else to understand what's going on inside of you.

To recover your balance and to get back on your feet will require you to search within yourself for strength and hope. No one else will be able to give you satisfactory answers to the questions that dominate your thoughts.

Your journey through grief will have many aspects in common with others who have also had terrible losses. You will not respond exactly like any other person. You are a unique person, and your grieving will reflect your uniqueness.

Cry if you are hurting, or allow yourself to feel anger if that is where you are. Feeling these emotions is proof you are human. The best thing to do is simply allow them to flow. Don't think you have to "keep it together" for anyone else, not even for the benefit of the children. If you want to talk about it until you lose your voice, then do it with anyone who will listen. If you want to cry, then cry. Don't hurry through your pain. Allow yourself to do what you think you need to do from day to day. The greater the loss, the more time required to recover. Recovering from Jeff's death is taking so much longer than it did for any other loss I've experienced to date.

Things to Try for Relief and Healing

- Within the first 24 to 48 hours after the death, periods of exercise alternated with relaxation will alleviate some physical reactions. Try moving to music or walk for 20 to 30 minutes.

- Don't make any "big" life changes (if possible).

- Avoid numbing the pain with the overuse of drugs or alcohol.

- Be kind to yourself.

- Treat yourself like you would another grieving person.

- Remember to eat a well-balanced diet.

- Get plenty of rest and sleep.

- You may or may not cry often, but when you do, realize it is okay. Don't fight the tears.

- Take care of yourself physically.

- Go to your doctor for a checkup.

- Find comfort in your family and friends, but don't expect them to meet all of your needs, because they are also grieving.

- Reach out and spend time with others. People do care.

- Retelling what happened is okay, because remembering your loved one and the experience of their death is healthy.

- Structure your time.

  - Keep busy but be sure the activity is worthwhile.

  - This is an excellent time to focus on your family and the loved one you lost.

- As you share your feelings, remember to ask about the feelings of others.

- Keep a journal. Write your way through those sleepless hours.

- Realize those around you are under pressure; try not to overreact to what is said and done.

- Don't be afraid to ask for help because we all need support.

- Join a support group.

- Remember grieving takes time, and your experiences and emotions can recur.

- Be patient with yourself and allow yourself to heal at your own pace.

According to Elisabeth Kübler-Ross, a renowned psychiatrist, there are five stages of grief: denial, anger, bargaining, depression and acceptance. Although these stages are common to the process of grief, they don't appear in a predictable order. Emotions will be random, sometimes overwhelming, and unique. Whatever emotions cause you to feel, try to remember that it's okay to feel how you are feeling.

Denial and Isolation

Denial and shock help us to contend with difficulties and make survival possible. Denial helps us to manage grief; it is the brain's way of letting in only what it can handle. Rationalizing overwhelming emotions is a normal response because it is a natural defense mechanism and it buffers shock. This is usually a temporary reaction that helps sustain us through the first wave of pain. In the first seven to ten days after a major loss you will probably feel stunned, shocked and overwhelmed. You may feel frozen or hysterical. Either way, you will have a difficult time later remembering much of what took place. Whatever your initial outward reaction, you will have a certain numbness inside. Your emotional system has shut down for the time being.

Denial can be either a conscious or unconscious refusal to accept what really happened, or the reality of the circumstances. In this stage, the world becomes meaningless and overwhelming: life makes no sense. When we are in a state of shock and denial, we become numb. We wonder how we can move on, if we can move on, or why we should go on. We try to find ways to get through each day.

Although living in denial may be necessary for a time, at some point a decision to move beyond the denial must be made. This doesn't mean you will stop grieving fully; it means your healing process has begun. As you accept the reality of death and begin to ask yourself questions, you are beginning the healing process. You are becoming stronger, and the denial is beginning to fade, and the feelings you were denying will begin to emerge. Remember, if you spend too long denying your loss, you will be unable to move forward with life.

Anger

As the shielding effects of denial and isolation begin to wane, reality and its associated pain begin to emerge as anger. This anger may be directed at yourself, others, or even those who are close to you. The anger may even be directed toward the dying or deceased. Feeling anger toward a lost one is not uncommon, but this feeling is further intensified for survivors of suicide because suicide can be perceived as the ultimate "Screw You" to those left behind.

Anyone who mourns the loss of a loved one may feel anger at being powerless in the face of his or her death, or anger at some real or perceived culprit. Those who mourn a suicide know the identity of the responsible person, and who would not feel rage toward the human being who put an end to the life of someone we have affection for, the human being who destroyed everyone around us? Many are reluctant to see their loved one in this harsh light, but the idea is there in our subconscious and at the heart of our depression. You may wake up in the morning, hoping to find you have been dreaming, only to realize yet again that what happened is no dream. Your loss is real, and it is permanent. Virtually every bereaved person is angry. The difference for survivors of suicide loss is that they are more aware of their anger, and it is often more intense than it is for those whose losses are from natural causes.

If you feel anger toward the deceased, let it out, because it is a fundamental part of your recovery process. You won't feel anger toward them forever. Expressing your anger will help you release it. You can then begin to incorporate positive feelings and happy thoughts of your lost loved one.

More than a few survivors feel the necessity for a guilty party, again out of a reluctance to hand over culpability to the suicide victim. "This is the doctor's responsibility." "His wife/mother/brother pushed him to it." "If only there was a better program…" Many even channel their anger into campaigns against some perceived cultural evil that is responsible for the loved one's death. While these people seem to have a productive focal point for their pain, they are only prolonging the agony for themselves by not coming to grips with the truth of their loved one's suicide. Their way back to contentment is made longer and rockier by misdirected rage.

Do you feel wrong about yearning for and missing your loved one? Most likely you don't; what you feel guilty about is your outrage. Are you angry with the person who died by suicide or are you angry about the decision they made to end their life?

It is not unheard of to grapple with opposing feelings of anger and sadness after losing someone to suicide. Realize it is common to feel anger toward the person that died by suicide and at the same time feel overwhelming sadness. They made a fatal decision that will affect the remainder of your life, leaving you to pick up the parts and deal with the outcome. Feeling guilty is normal after feeling anger toward the deceased.

Suicide is an act of violence, not only against the person who died but also against those left behind. Their death leaves an unusually intense feeling of abandonment, because the death was their choice. They decided to leave you behind. Chances are you are angry at the decision, not the person; and it was your beloved who made the choice, not you. If you knew what they were planning, you would have done everything you could have to prevent it.

Anger is a significant stage of the healing process. Be prepared to feel your anger, even though it may seem without end. The more you feel it, the more it will begin to diffuse and the more you will recover. There are several other feelings below the rage, and you will get to them in due time, but anger is the feeling we are most accustomed to managing. Underneath anger is pain, your pain. Anger is power, and it can be a support system, giving temporary structure to the emptiness of loss.

At first, grief may seem like being lost at sea with no attachment to anything. Then you get furious at someone, maybe a person who did not make an appearance at the funeral, maybe a person who is not around, perhaps a person who is different now that your loved one has died. Without any warning, you have a structure: your anger toward them. The anger becomes a scaffold over the empty abyss, a bond from you to them. Anger is something to hold onto because a link made from the power of anger feels better than nothing. We ordinarily know more about suppressing anger than feeling it. The anger is evidence of the intensity of your love.

Give yourself permission to be angry at what they did, because it was not okay. Then get back in the game. That is the truth. You experienced a devastating loss, but you did not choose it. Give yourself permission to carry on. Recognize anger is okay; it is what is done with the anger that is relevant.

Bargaining

A common reaction to feeling helpless and vulnerable is the need to regain a semblance of control through bargaining. Before a loss, it feels as though you would do anything if only your loved one could be saved. You may plead with some higher power, "I will never be angry at my son again if you will let him live." Promising a higher power we will be a better person, quitting an unhealthy habit, or promising we would treat the lost loved one differently exemplifies the bargaining process. After a loss, bargaining may take the form of a short term peace agreement. "What if I dedicate the remainder of my life to serving others? Then can I wake up and recognize this has all been an undesirable nightmare?"

We get lost in a labyrinth of "If only…" or "What if…" declarations. We want life put back to what it was; we want our loved one put back. We want to go back in time: stumble on the disease sooner, recognize the infection more quickly, and stop the suicide from occurring if only, if only, if only. Guilt is often bargaining's companion. Bargaining causes us to find blame in ourselves and what we "believe" we could have done differently. We may even negotiate with the pain. We will do anything not to feel the pain of this loss. We remain in the past, making every effort to negotiate our way out of the hurt. People often assume the stages only last for a few weeks or months. They forget the stages are responses to emotions that can last for moments or hours as we pitch in and out of one and then another. We don't enter and pull out of each stage in a linear manner. We may experience one, then another, and back again to the first one.

Bargaining doesn't provide a sustainable solution because it implies there is something that could be done to change history. The unfortunate truth is we will never see the loved one again, and thinking about how things might be different today if only things were done differently in the past adds to the torturous experience. These thoughts and fantasies just don't fit with the present reality. Bargaining is a thin line of defense to protect us from the pain we are facing.

Depression

After bargaining, our attention moves into the present moment. Empty feelings present themselves, and grief enters our lives on a profound level, deeper than we ever imagined was possible. The depressive stage feels as if it will last forever, but it is necessary to recognize this depression is not a sign of mental illness. Depression is an appropriate response to a significant loss—especially a suicide loss. We withdraw from life, left in a haze of extreme sadness, wondering if there is any point in going on.

Depression after a loss is generally regarded as an unnatural state, a problem to be repaired, something to snap out of. The first question to ask yourself is whether the situation you are in is depressing. The loss of a loved one is an extremely heartbreaking situation, and depression is a common and appropriate response. Not experiencing depression after a loved one dies would be surprising. When a loss fully settles in your heart, the recognition that your loved one is gone and is not coming back is understandably upsetting. If grief is a form of healing, then depression is one of the many essential steps along the way.

Attempting to cheer up a person who is in this stage is not recommended, because it is a critical time for grieving, which must be processed. Feeling sadness, regret, fear, and uncertainty is understandable when going through this stage because it shows the person has begun to accept the situation.

Acceptance

Losing someone to a "conventional" death, while challenging, doesn't interfere with pleasant memories of him or her. Suicide survivors often feel separated and "divorced" from the memory of their lost loved one because they opted to end their own lives. To our rational minds this is an unimaginable act, and it places us in a state of opposition with them. At some point, we have to reconcile with them, and somehow, we need to achieve this alone because no one can do it for us.

Unfortunately, this level of acceptance usually takes an awfully long time to achieve. Accepting a loss is the most important step of your recovery. It is at this point that you will again take full charge of your life and full responsibility for your feelings. A noticeable sense of balance is coming back into your life when you can accept that your loss is real and permanent. It represents a giant step toward full recovery.

Although acceptance is essential to healing for the survivor of suicide, it is a deceptively easy concept. Most of us operate under the theory that we are already accepting the death. After all, only a deluded few would fail to believe the incident occurred. Accepting a suicide means not only acknowledging the underlying reality, but also accepting the elements and the repercussions of it without embellishing them with conjured-up ideas, either negative or positive.

Case in point, you might have to accept that your loved one lost a remarkably long struggle with depression. If you were to embellish this fact either positively—by denying the reality such a profound emotional illness could have existed within them—or negatively—by unfairly holding yourself accountable for not having remedied them of it—then you are not really accepting the suicide for what it is: a terrible event that, while entirely unwished for, was beyond the control of you and those around you. In this way, acceptance is the process of separating myth from reality.

Not everyone is fortunate enough to reach a point of true acceptance for his or her loss. Death may be sudden and unexpected, or we may never see beyond our anger or denial. Wanting to know as much about your loved one's suicide as possible is common. Seeking these answers is an essential part of your grief. Some people investigate the circumstances of the suicide with the zeal of an FBI agent. Examine and reexamine your loved one's suicide as much or as little as needed. Be prepared to accept the distinct possibility that many of the answers you seek may be unknowable. Only after you have drained your deductive abilities can you at long last let go of the "Why?" There will come a time when you will hopefully accept that a satisfying reason for your loss may not exist. Even if it did, it would not change what has happened. Once you can let go of "Why?" you have taken a significant step toward acceptance.

Be aware that moving on with your life can bring its own level of guilt. Whether it is returning to the simple routine of daily living or embarking on new adventures in life, survivors often feel as if this is some slight to the person they've lost. "How can I live knowing they are not here?" As we try to incorporate the trauma of losing a person we love in such a violent and painful manner, we yearn for the return of a routine. Your strength lies in knowing that, while your lost loved one has chosen death, you have chosen life—and life is a gift honored by living. You should not feel guilty because you have a desire to heal. It is not a betrayal to the memory of your loved one.

Acceptance is often confused with the idea of being "all right" or "okay" with what has taken place. This is not the case. Most people don't ever feel okay or all right about the loss of a loved one. This stage is about accepting the fact that the loved one is actually gone and recognizing that this new reality is the permanent reality. We will never like this fact or make it okay, but eventually we accept it. We learn to live with it because it is the new normal with which we must learn to live. We must try to live now in a world where the loved one is missing. In resisting this new normal, at first many people want to preserve life as it was before a loved one died. In time, through bits and pieces of acceptance, however, we realize we cannot preserve the past intact because it has been forever altered and we must readjust. We must learn to reorganize functions, reassign them to others, or take them on ourselves. The challenge of grief recovery after any loss is to establish a new normal for life.

Finding acceptance may be having more good days than unpleasant ones. As we begin to live again and enjoy life, we often think that in doing so, we are betraying the loved one. We can never replace what has been lost, but we can create new connections, new relationships, and new interdependencies. Instead of denying our feelings, we listen to our needs; we change, we grow, and we adapt. We may begin to reach out to others and get involved in their lives. We invest in friendships and in a relationship with ourselves.

Acceptance is the return of self-esteem and the reversal of personal losses. You may develop new skills and begin to put your life back together. You let go of the guilt, sadness and heartbreak through forgiveness. You remove emotional energy from the loss and reinvest it elsewhere. You find the new you. You begin to transform the loss into a new opportunity. You begin to laugh again!

Accept that you couldn't alter what occurred, and did the best you could do with what you knew at the moment. If you are burdening yourself with misplaced guilt, you are in effect confining yourself to an emotional prison. The bars of an emotional jail are made out of guilt, anger, bitterness and resentment. What people don't know is that this is a prison that locks from the inside. There is not anybody that can allow you out of your prison except for you. The challenge of dealing with a loved one's suicide is one of the most troublesome calamities anyone ever has to grapple with, but make no mistake: you must face it. If you try to ignore it, you may only be delaying an even deeper pain. There are those who have suffered breakdowns decades after a suicide because they refused or were banned from talking about such a thing. You get out of bed every day and decide what to think. If you have chosen to bear the burden of guilt, shame, anger and misery everywhere you go, what would happen if you decided, "I cannot change what happened—so I'd better accept it, and understand that the life that I have today, tomorrow and the next day is going to be a function of what I choose"?

In our bereavement, individuals spend varying lengths of time on each of the stages, and the stages don't appear in the same order for everyone. Frequently people move from one stage to another before achieving any healing of their loss. We begin to live again, but we cannot do so until we have given grief its time.

CHILDREN AND GRIEF

Death is the one and only sure thing in all of life, and is also one of life's greatest uncertainties. When speaking about death, there are no simple explanations, particularly with children. Nearly all people are uncertain of how to tell their children, or of what the child's reaction will be. Children undergo loss for all practical purposes on a daily basis through divorce, loss of friends, changing schools, or the death of a pet. The following information is intended to assist you with helping a child cope with the death of a loved one, and it may also be useful when dealing with any life loss.

It is specifically because young children don't know what death is all about that they particularly need us to discuss it with them. When someone dies, children feel the loss as much as any adult. They just don't have the words to tell us about their feelings. Remember that while adults internalize their feelings, children act them out. Their vocabulary may be limited, but their behavior can reveal volumes about their feelings. When adults try to shelter and protect them from the experience, children turn to their own imaginations, which often suggest a situation even worse than the real one. Young children often assume that they are somehow to blame for the loss. They are used to thinking in terms of blame for spilled drinks and broken toys. It's easy for children to interpret the combination of adult silence and sadness as a disappointment in them.

Death has become to some extent a taboo matter in society, and there is an inclination to avoid it. Often, because we know the sorrow and pain, we want to protect children, at times to the extent we don't tell them about a death. A death disrupts a child's emotional life, and all family members are affected. Children see something is wrong, and they will experience grief one way or another. Therefore, it is vital we speak truthfully with our children.

How we communicate with a child about death depends on many things, such as their age, temperament, and connection with the one who has died. However, it is vital we provide the child with clear and direct information while remaining open to their questions. We should give the child responses to build on in future discussions, not ones that will have to be unlearned. Children will create their own fantasy explanations for unanswered questions, with these fantasies often being more terrifying than the reality. Children take what we say verbatim, so it is best to avoid metaphorical speech such as "passed away," "went to sleep," etc.

Explain death on a level they can comprehend. Young ones can take in only small volumes of information, so the explanation should be short and straightforward. The older the child, the more information they can receive and process. Most children are curious about the physical characteristics of death, and describing the death concretely reduces the confusion. For example, talk about the absence of natural life functions. When a person dies, their heart doesn't beat, they don't breathe, talk, eat or think. Until about nine years of age, it is difficult for children to understand the finality of death. They may frequently ask you the same questions before the answers become fact to them. Talking with children is difficult, because we don't have all the answers, and that is okay, because there is not always an answer for every question. If we can be as open, honest and comfortable with emotions as possible, we make it much easier for children to discuss death and ask questions. This is significant because it lets us be aware of what they need and how we can help.

How Children Grieve

A child that is old enough to love someone is old enough to grieve their death. Everyone, including children, has their very own individual grief experience. Like adults, children experience trauma, sadness, fear, and guilt. We should not tell children how to feel. Similar to grown-ups, children are sensitive to feelings of helplessness, and feel uncertain about what has taken place and what the future holds. Children must generally receive their grief in doses. They find it challenging to manage prolonged exposure to grieving. One moment they may ask you a particular question regarding the death, and the next moment resume the game they were playing. Because a child's potential to feel develops long before their ability to verbalize emotions, their concerns and anxieties may not appear in straightforward questions but rather through play. Children will display a broad range of behavior and, because of cultural expectations and what they are taught, girls and boys may express feelings differently. Some children may regress emotionally and developmentally with tantrums, aggressive behavior or withdrawal.

Parents often become alarmed when their child doesn't seem to be grieving because they continue to play normally. Occasionally, like adults, children may need to be left alone, and we should respect their need for privacy. Often, children turn their anger and sorrow inward and become depressed and withdrawn.

Because the grief experience is a personal one, there is no incorrect way to grieve. We must be patient and accepting of children throughout this ongoing process. No matter what their behavior, a loving and supportive environment is essential for their emotional health.

Children & Funerals

A funeral is a time of sorrow, a day to honor the person who died, a moment to help comfort and support each other, and a time to affirm life will continue.

As a part of the healing process, children should be encouraged to attend the funeral. However, they should not be forced or made to feel guilty if they decide not to attend. In most cases, they will choose to attend if they are prepared for what to anticipate and they are given support. Be sure to explain to the child the reason for funerals. They can usually accept that it is a time for goodbye. This may also be a convenient time to explain the spiritual significance, according to your particular religious beliefs. If a child attends a funeral, an account of what will happen before, during, and after the service is needed. Children should also be made aware they will see people showing a wide range of emotions in expressing their feelings. If appropriate, children can also be encouraged to participate in the funeral process. Your funeral director can provide helpful information and answers to questions about children and funerals.

Needs of a Grieving Child

- Open, honest information regarding the death

- Saying goodbye to the deceased

- Participation in the funeral ritual, if they choose

- Reassurance basic needs will be met

- Consistency and routine in daily living

- An ongoing, loving and supportive environment where feelings and thoughts can be expressed openly

Bereaved children can and do grow through grief. A child's suffering is as powerful and intense as any adult's grief. Bereaved children must explore how they go on with their lives because they are forever changed by the death of a loved one. Help your children in their healing and development by providing a safe, loving and supportive environment. If you are open to them, your children will be your best teachers and let you know what they need.

MEN AND GRIEF

Current scientific research on the brain shows that men are functionally different from women. These differences account for many of the variations between how men and women process information and the feelings they have. Contending with grief and death is no exception. While men and women undergo the same grief, they will likely process and show it in distinctly different ways. Women often have an established network of friends and relationships, giving them an opportunity for deep personal sharing.

Until recently, men have been expected to be emotionally controlled and emotionless. Men tend to grieve alone and to show little about what they are feeling. Men don't share with each other like women do. This stereotypical male has to be strong, and often doesn't display emotion at the time of death of their loved ones. Most men deal with pain using the same strategies they use to deal with everything else, by controlling their emotions and relying on their own internal strengths. Men, therefore, don't react favorably when asked to do "grief work," which typically involves discussing the emotions associated with the loss. The problem is that keeping emotions bottled up inside significantly slows the healing process.

No matter what gender, we oscillate between positive and negative emotions, between waves of unhappiness about the loss and hope for the future. The loss of a loved one is a crushing experience both physically and psychologically, but symptoms for men are often intensified because many are reluctant to confront their feelings. Whether you are a man or a woman, you need to express your emotions.

Emotions can be intimidating because they are the least controllable aspect of your nature. Men in particular feel the need to be in charge. When a man begins confronting his emotions, his worst fears begin to be realized. Many men are simply not comfortable with talking about their feelings because they have been conditioned to keep their feelings hidden by society. In reality, expressing emotions is a sign of strength, because it means you are working through the emotions. The fact that, after a loss, it is more likely that a community will recognize a woman's feelings rather than a man's reinforces the reason they should keep their emotions inside. This often leads to lack of social support and exclusion from care, which further intensifies the suffering. Men who rarely express emotions during normal times often find they don't have the tools needed to express their grief in times of bereavement. Their ideas of how a man should behave can hinder the healthy expression of their emotions. Along with emotional issues there can be physical problems. Heart attacks, ulcers and cancer are a few of the ailments that can be created when the suffering stays within. There are also differences in the time men grieve, compared with women, and how long it takes to move on. This can be frustrating for men, who often seek the "quick-fix" approach. Many of society's stereotypes of how a grieving person should behave are based on the way women grieve. Here are some things men should keep in mind.

- You will grieve in your own custom.

- There is no how-to guide for how you should grieve.

- Your grief process is influenced by who you are, how you were raised, and your life experiences.

- You may not want to talk about it as often as those around you.

- You may use action instead of talking to work through your feelings.

- Working side by side may be an easier way to handle grief than communicating face to face.

- You may want to do your healing on your own and through your own inner strength.

- You may wish to take on the role of caretaker of those around you to help you manage your own grief.

- Grief is a process that will make you stronger.

- All people have a combination of both "masculine" and "feminine" characteristics that will affect their way of mourning.

While society may be changing, the lingering mentality of "Big boys don't cry" leads many men to try to avoid the grief process altogether. They may fear that showing their suffering will make them look weak. The problem is, not crying is inappropriate behavior that can put you at exceptional risk of physical and emotional illness. Those who want you to keep your grief in check are seeking their own comfort, not yours. To heal properly, you must show your grief without constraint, and for as long as it takes to release it. Big boys don't cry, but real men do. Women are smarter and healthier, not weaker, because they typically have an easier time crying. Crying is actually one of the healthiest things anyone can do. Studies have shown that tears of sadness have a different chemical makeup than tears of joy. Tears of sadness release substances that have a calming effect. It is no myth that you will feel better after a good cry. Some studies indicate that tears are washing toxins out of the body, which means not crying is holding these poisons inside. Tears are a sign that you are on the way to recovery.

Some of the common ways men try to cover up their feelings of grief are silence, secrecy, anger, action or addiction.

While every man's experience of grief will vary, there are some things that all men who are grieving have in common, and so the following tips are offered to men who are grieving, and those that are attempting to assist them. Men who express, release or sufficiently work through their grief are the exception rather than the rule.

Men who share their grief will experience many advantages to their emotional and physical health and relationships. They will also experience more happiness and energy.

Undergo your grief in your own way. As long as you are not bringing harm to yourself or others, there is no right or wrong way to grieve. Grief is an individualized experience for everyone. The way you grieve may not be what you expected for yourself or what others expect. Although countless men have experienced grief before you, each man's grief response to suffering is different. Honestly experiencing grief is a critical step towards healing. Your journey of grief will be uniquely your own.

Give yourself plenty of time to grieve. After the passing of a loved one, there are usually many arrangements to be made and other mourners to be cared for. While no man wants to avoid his duty, it is necessary to allow time to grieve. Grief's unexpected turns will throw you repeatedly. You may notice that for every step forward, you take at minimum one step back. The grieving process typically takes longer than ever imagined. Remember that what you are feeling is not only expected—it is necessary. The uncertain timing and varied combinations of emotions that arise during grief can leave you confused and discouraged. Your emotions not only hit hard, but they can also occur at unexpected moments, which makes the effect seem even worse. Being aware of the random nature of your feelings will help you to stand strong during each new torrent. The emotions will be like a ride that you cannot get off of. Stay on the ride, because you cannot rush the process. Grief cannot be rushed. Other men may advise you to "get over it" or to "get back on the horse." Keep in mind that you have an insight into the grieving process these men don't have. You know the extent of the grieving process is different for each person. You know that you have to let the grieving process take place, because if you rush it, you will only prolong the pain.

Each time one of these feelings comes back, it is a sign you are forging ahead. If you want to recover from sorrow you must go through it; you cannot go around it. Because it is an appropriate response to loss, grief is not a bad word! It is not a sign of weakness. Grief isn't something to avoid at all costs and get over as quickly as possible. Joy is not necessarily better than grief. It may be more fun to feel happiness, but that doesn't mean it is better. If something good is happening, it is appropriate to be happy. If you have experienced loss, it is equally appropriate to be sad. Don't look at healing as a goal you can only achieve at the end of a process. Each step you take is part of the healing. Your journey through grief cannot be compared to another person's journey.

Pay attention to harmful behaviors and emotions. While experiencing anger is normal, it is necessary to manage anger so that it doesn't harm others. Grieving men are more apt to develop problems with alcohol or other substances; their use should be carefully monitored. Know when to go in search of assistance. Counseling may be helpful but is not required. However, if you have earnest thoughts of suicide or self-harm, seek psychological attention right away.

Call on your male friends. Other men, particularly other men who have had a comparable loss, can be some of your greatest sources of comfort.

If you are employed, it is beneficial to go back to work as soon as you can. Let the relevant people know that, for the next few weeks or months, you may not perform as efficiently as you did before. Assure these people—your supervisor, business associates, or other contacts—that your performance will return to normal, and believe yourself that it will. At times, you may find that a day is going along reasonably smoothly when suddenly something calls you back to the intensity of your loss and grief. At that point, you will need to go home or take a break until you can regain your composure.

The most crucial thing is that each person finds a safe way to express his or her grief. While some may be comfortable in a group setting, others may be more at ease working through their grief on their own, or with the support of educational books and websites. Some use music, art or writing to help them grieve. Some may use rituals to bring them comfort. As time passes, the methods employed to contend with grief will vary.

HELPING A GRIEVING MAN

Be there. Simply knowing you are free to support him has a positive effect on a grieving man. Even if you believe it goes without saying, make it a point to tell him you are available and prepared to help.

Be prepared to listen. A grieving man may or may not want to speak about his struggles. If he does, lend an ear openly. Generally, the less you say the better. Avoid dispensing advice or problem-solving unless asked.

Allow him to face his suffering his way. Don't set timetables for his grief or require him to mourn in a certain way. Follow his lead in how you can help.

Take care of yourself. Seeing a friend in the depths of despair is difficult and takes its toll mentally. Make sure to provide for your personal care, so you have the energy required to help your friend.

Know when to seek help. Most men will continue through the grieving process without the need for counseling; however, if your friend threatens or attempts suicide, harms or threatens to harm themselves or others, or develops a substance abuse problem, advise them to seek treatment immediately.

HELPING THE BEREAVED

The loss of a loved one by suicide is shocking, painful and often unexpected. The pain that emanates from this type of loss can be intense, complex and exceptionally long term. There is no given duration to being bereaved by suicide. Survivors of suicide come to realize their lives will never return to how they were; they must adapt to life without their loved one. Many people search for the right words to say when they discover that someone they know has suffered a loss. Others say the first thing that comes to mind. Most people have no idea what it is like, and their well-intentioned advice or words of comfort often cause more pain and suffering.

The right words of encouragement can make all the difference to someone suffering a loss; the wrong ones can hurt. Before attempting to help, you must overcome any preconceptions you may have about suicide or the suicide victim. Suicide is an uncomfortable subject, but the people left behind are in significant pain and in need of your compassion. The most powerful and useful thing you can do is to listen without judgment, criticism, or prejudice.

When you do, offer words of comfort. Be sure to avoid phrases similar to the following examples.

- At least she lived a long life; many people die young.

- He is in a better place now.

- She brought this on herself.

- There is a reason for everything.

- Aren't you over him yet? He has been dead for a while now.

- You can still have another child.

- She was such a selfless person that God wanted her to be with him.

- I know how you feel.

- She did what she came here to do and it was her time to go.

- Be strong.

The reason these comments hurt is that they want to fix the loss, even though this is not possible. The comments are about our anxiety and are directive in nature. They are trying to rationalize or explain loss when there is no explanation that eases suffering. The comments come across as judgmental, and they are not about the griever. Above all, they minimize feelings of loss and put an artificial timeline on recovering from the loss.

The most helpful things you could say or do for someone grieving a loss would be more like the following.

- I'm so sorry for your loss.

- I wish I had the right words; just know I care.

- I don't know how you feel, but I'm here to help in any way I can.

- You and your loved one will be in my thoughts and prayers.

- My favorite memory of your loved one is…

- I'm a phone call away.

- We all need help at times like this; I'm here for you.

- I'm usually up early or late, if you need anything.

- Give a hug instead of saying something.

- Or say nothing; simply stay with the person.

The reason these are more helpful is that they are encouraging, but not trying to "fix" it. They focus on the feelings the person is experiencing. Also, they are non-active, not telling anyone what to do. These comments illustrate that you cannot make it better, and you are not asking them to change how they feel. They recognize loss and they don't set a time limit.

Avoid remarks like "I know how you feel" unless you, too, have survived a loss through suicide. You cannot lead someone through his or her grief. Their grieving process will be unique. Your company and unconditional listening are what they want the most. Above all, don't tell them how they should act, how they should feel, or that they should feel better by now.

The worst that could happen has already happened! You can't fix it, but you can comfort.

What can I say?

The most thoughtful and honest words are "I'm so sorry." You may wish to continue with "They will be missed" or even "I don't know what to say." If you were close to the deceased person, or spent a fun or significant time with them, share that with the family. Every positive mention, every antic, humorous story or reinforcing action involving the person who died is invaluable to the surviving family.

Some have asked me if they should say the word "suicide." I tell them the cause of death was suicide, that is what it is called, and it is okay to say the word. Often "killed himself" or "ended their own life" is used, but there is no soft, gentle way of saying, "suicide." I suggest not using "committed suicide." "Committed" implies a crime. Suicide is not a crime, and it is never appropriate to use offensive phrases defining suicide. This is of course a relic of the relatively recent past, when suicide was considered a crime. For many families, this term is offensive and upsetting. Saying "died by suicide" is much more sensitive and much more accurate.

Can I ask "What Happened?"

If you are a close friend or extended family member, you may want to say, "Do you want to tell me what happened?" If you suspect that question will be viewed as intrusive, be guided by what the bereaved is saying. Suicide is so shocking, devastating and usually unexpected, that family members may have a need to talk about what took place, relating in detail the last words, actions, or what they found or saw. If you cannot handle the details of the death, don't put yourself in a place to hear them. Don't tell the grieving not to talk about the death or the circumstances surrounding the death. Talking is cathartic and a key component in the grieving and healing process. You are there to support and help. Listening may be your most thoughtful gift.

Should I say the deceased person's name?

There will never be a time when the family will not need to hear the name of the one who has died. Although the person is no longer living, that person is still a part of the family. When the family speaks of the deceased in the past tense, the support community is encouraged to do so, as well. By listening as the family speaks, you will be guided in your own style of addressing the death.

What Can You Do to Help?

- Be there.

- Anticipate and respond to need.

- Assure water and tissues are at hand for the bereaved.

- A hug is appropriate and generally welcomed. However, there are those who don't want to be touched, so you may need to ask if you can give a hug before doing so.

- You may shed tears in the presence of the newly bereaved, and that is okay, albeit not excessively. Tears express genuine empathy, and knowing the death touches the hearts of others lends a bit of comfort and solace to the bereaved.

- Depending upon the situation, you may help by tending young surviving children, answering calls and recording callers, preparing meals, keeping records of gifts of flowers and food, performing yard or house work, making arrangements (i.e. funeral, travel, room accommodations), helping select funeral attire (laundry, cleaners etc.) and, at a later time, writing thank-you notes, helping file insurance or social security claims, or seeking legal counsel. The family may designate a spokesperson to address the cause and circumstances of the death with callers. Providing facts restores a degree of control to the immediate survivors and lessens opportunity for rumors and gossip.

- In accordance with the boundaries of your relationship, discourage efforts of confidentiality regarding the cause of death. Secrecy severely distorts and complicates healthy grieving and can create family conflict and breaches. Increasingly, survivor families are openly designating contributions to suicide prevention organizations.

- Find out whether there is a support group for suicide bereaved nearby, provide contact information to the survivor, and offer to attend with them if this is permissible to the group leader.

- There are books and websites that provide support articles for suicide bereaved. A book or downloaded articles offers another avenue for validating their pain and assuring them they are not alone on this grief journey.

- If you know a long-term suicide survivor willing to offer empathy and support, ask the newly bereaved family if a call from the seasoned survivor would be helpful.

- In the weeks following the death, when all the "tragedy-focused" activity has subsided, the survivor needs calls, notes of support, dinner brought in, visits, and distracting activities. Invitations may not be accepted, but the fact that they are extended is reinforcing.

Is it helpful to share faith-based views or previous experience with suicide?

No, refrain from interpreting God's view on suicide. If the bereaved has questions regarding suicide with regard to sin and religion, ask a clergy person to respond. Sharing judgmental beliefs about suicide are not practical, nor, in the immediate aftermath, is it helpful or appropriate to share your personal struggles with mental illness, suicidal ideation or attempts.

Are there topics to avoid?

Sharing the tragedies of others with newly bereaved persons is not helpful. Don't try to cheer the grieving person. There is a time for that, but the time is not in the days following the death. Be as natural and positive as possible. Deflect statements that perpetuate bias and misconception around the issue of suicide.

How long will it be before they are healed and back to normal?

Adjusting to the loss of someone dearly loved is a life work in progress. Grief is not time-limited or measurable. Like a snowflake, grief is unique with each individual. The old routine is gone; a new normal will evolve. The lives of the surviving family are forever changed by this tragedy, but eventually the initial raging grief gentles into sorrow and regret that is tolerable and manageable. Be alert for indications of excessive guilt, anger, or language of wanting to die. While it is not unusual or uncommon for suicide bereaved to speak of not wanting to live, it can also be a red flag. If such talk persists, it is advisable to research available mental health professionals with expertise in grief, perhaps certified in EMDR, and encourage an immediate appointment to ensure the safety of the bereaved and the peace of mind of all who care for them.

SUGGESTIONS FOR SURVIVORS

Along my long and winding road toward healing from Jeff's suicide I've collected so many pieces of advice. This information has helped me gather the strength to get out of bed in the morning and function for yet another day. I felt I would never laugh or feel carefree ever again in my life. We all deal with suicide differently. Some have anger, some have sorrow, and some experience forgiveness and compassion, but we all experience loss.

Foremost it is essential to realize you can survive this loss. Even if you may not believe it is possible right now, you can. The emotional journey of enduring Jeff's suicide has been the most difficult experience in my life, but I've survived and learned from it. Your emotional survival depends on your ability to learn how to contend with the tragedy of surviving a loved one's suicide. Having suicidal thoughts during this time is not uncommon; but it doesn't mean you will act on those thoughts. What you are enduring is one of the most harrowing ordeals possible in the human experience. The risk of suicide in surviving families is greater than families that have not endured this type of tragedy. This may be because our loved one's death has made the concept of suicide real in our lives, making it extremely common for those left behind to have suicidal feelings themselves. However, you must balance your fear with the understanding that suicide is usually preceded by a history of clinical depression. If you share this characteristic with your loved one, then you may have a reason to seek professional help. However, you now know better than anyone the pain and damage suicide can create in the lives of those we love. The fact that you are reading a book like this one shows that your desire to heal and live far outweighs any desire you have to end your life.

Along with the grief, you are riding an out-of-control roller coaster of emotions, fraught with sadness and confusion that is in many ways unique to survivors of suicide. Remember to take one moment or one day at a time. The suicide irrevocably transforms us. Our world explodes, and we are never the same. Many, if not most, of us will adapt, eventually learning to navigate on the ground that we no longer trust to be steady. We gradually come to accept that our questions will never be answered. We try not to torture ourselves for having failed to predict the oncoming tragedy and failed to prevent our loved one from taking their life.

Allow yourself to struggle with the "why" questions until you no longer feel the need to know "why"—or at least until you are satisfied with partial answers. Why didn't we see our loved ones were depressed? Why didn't we force them to get help? Why didn't we return their last phone call? Why did we say such horrible things to them during our previous argument? The worst thing about "why" questions is that the person asking really doesn't want the only answer that makes sense. Questions that begin with "why" reflect a desperate yearning for meaning and purpose. They look for someone or something to blame for the loss. They are sure there is some reason for what happened. They think they might feel better and hurt less if only they could discover that reason.

You may feel overwhelmed by the magnitude of your feelings. You are not crazy, you are grieving: it is both healthy and normal to repeat your questions repeatedly, and to experience unusually strong emotions until you are ready to let them go. The decision to die by suicide creates such a sense of utter helplessness for those left behind. Not only do survivors feel helpless and ineffectual in the face of suicide, we also feel hurt and betrayed by the loved ones for making such an irrevocable decision without turning to us for assistance. Anger, guilt, confusion and forgetfulness are extremely common responses. To maintain a sense of control we often blame the deaths of our loved ones on the actions we took or the omissions we made.

Avoid people who want to tell you what or how to feel. Friends and family may not offer the help you need. This experience will teach you who your friends are. A casual acquaintance may turn out to be your most faithful supporter, while a lifelong friend might turn their back on you. Lean on the people who are ready, willing, and able to help you rather than getting angry with those that cannot.

Time heals, but time alone cannot heal the suicide survivor. You must use that time to heal yourself and rely on the help and support of others. Although it might take years to restore your emotional well-being, you can be assured of one thing: it will get easier.

People will say insensitive things because suicide is widely misunderstood, and people will feel awkward at offering you comfort. This is only human nature, and while it would be fantastic if people rose above it, try not to be too hard on those who cannot. If you come across someone who seems determined to upset you with morbid curiosity, their own egotistical theories, or some kind of "guilt trip," simply bypass them by saying, "I'd rather not talk about it right now," and avoid speaking with them in the future.

Letting go of grief can be difficult to do when there are still unresolved issues that need to be worked through. This can keep you from moving forward, and it can hinder your recovery. Processing pain and hurt and allowing ourselves to feel anger and grief can help release bottled-up feelings and cope with them in a healthy way. In situations where there has been significant loss, trauma, or abuse, counseling might be especially helpful. In order to let go of the pain, you have to stop blaming the past. You must take responsibility for your own recovery. That is when healing begins. You can't change the past, but you can do something about today and the rest of your life.

Today is all anyone has, and today is the only place happiness, wholeness, and contentment can exist. To live one day at a time, you must fully experience life. One day, one hour, one moment at a time. So much is lost right here and now when we focus on the past or the future.

Learn to live for today and plan for tomorrow. Planning for tomorrow requires setting goals for the future. When you don't set any goals, you have nothing drawing you forward. Setting goals gives you a sense of purpose. Letting go of the past helps you live with new hope and purpose.

Give yourself plenty of time to heal, and when you are ready to start letting go, it doesn't mean you will forget about the one you lost. Realize that moving on doesn't mean you have to stop loving the person you lost, it only means your love for them has changed. You can expect many setbacks along the way; your emotions will ebb and flow. You might have a few weeks in a row where you feel better and then your grief will return without warning. This is normal, so don't be discouraged. You will experience ups and downs, but generally, contending with your loss will become easier as time passes.

You will come across painful reminders along the way. A favorite song on the radio, a smell, or even a photograph can bring on sudden feelings of sadness or even the sensation you are reliving the experience of the suicide. When this happens, try not to panic. Get away from the reminder if you need to and focus on positive thoughts. The awful truth is that you will never truly "get over" your loss. The goal is to go through the grief and to accept your life as it is now, forever changed.

Have you ever found yourself overreacting to a minor disappointment? Do you have moments when you are easily offended and short-tempered without knowing why? Such behavior often results when some comparatively minor loss experience brings the gathered energy of a number of buried losses from the past—losses that were not sufficiently acknowledged at the time they happened. Thinking back on these losses is not enjoyable, but it is necessary if they are to be healed. It should come as no surprise that we sometimes cry over a seemingly minor disappointment. Our accumulation of loss experiences is like that. We store them up over time until something happens to trigger the outpouring of all our pent-up feelings. Norman Cousins said, "Death is not the enemy. Living in constant fear of it is."

Experiencing real physical reactions to your grief—such as headaches, loss of appetite, or the inability to sleep—is not uncommon. During this period of increased emotions, it is advisable to put off major decisions until a later time. Be patient with yourself and others who may not understand. Although you will never be the same again, you will learn how to survive and even go beyond surviving.

Don't be afraid to cry, because tears are a crucial part of the healing process. They are a sign that you are confronting your grief.

If you cannot move on past the grieving process because the grief is your current connection to the deceased, ask yourself how awful it is that your cherished loved one is being remembered as a legacy of pain that you choose to carry around. You're focusing on the moment they died instead of on the moments they lived and the joy they brought to your life. Isn't that a terrible burden to put on your loved one?

The desire to laugh is beneficial, and it is a powerful tool for relieving stress because it can dissipate anger, depression and other negative emotions. Laughter can help promote feelings of optimism and resiliency that will help you bounce back from surviving through such trying times. Laughter is like good medicine that brings healing to the body and mind. Some report that the average child laughs about 150 times a day while the average adult laughs 4 to 8 times a day. Although you cannot force yourself to have fun, you can choose to do things that once brought you pleasure. You may not feel like it, but push yourself and do it anyway. Taking the simple steps in doing something that you once enjoyed can help you feel better than you would expect. You may begin to feel reconnected with life and others. It can boost your mood and help you to feel more energetic.

Everyone needs a good balance of enjoyable activities in their lives. Think of what helped you in the past. It could be something creative like music, art, or writing, or a sport or other hobby. Whether you do something alone or with others, keeping yourself occupied with good activities is a healthy coping tool for depression. Also, it is never too late to try to learn something new. Sometimes people get stuck in a rut of doing the same things because they assume they won't like it, or they're afraid to try something unfamiliar to them. Trying something new can help you to discover new interests that can help bring balance to your life.

Some people don't eat right when they are depressed. They may not have much of an appetite, so their bodies aren't provided with the proper nutrients. Others use food for comfort, and they crave food that isn't good for them. What we eat not only impacts our overall physical health, but it also affects our mood. Brain chemicals associated with mood (neurotransmitters—dopamine, serotonin, and norepinephrine) are regulated by what we eat. For example, complex carbohydrates (fruits, vegetables, whole grains) are known to increase serotonin production. A diet that's very low in complex carbs can deplete serotonin and cause depression. Foods high in protein help to increase production of dopamine and norepinephrine, which promote alertness; whereas foods high in saturated fats can lead to fatigue and lethargy. Sugars initially increase energy, but quickly lead to fatigue. A deficiency in vitamins and minerals has been associated with low mood, particularly the B vitamins. Some medications deplete the body of certain vitamins that can affect mood. Caffeine, alcohol, and tobacco all contribute to mood. Alcohol depresses the central nervous system and actually increases depression symptoms. A healthy, well-balanced diet contributes to good physical as well as mental health.

Getting enough sleep is necessary for optimal mental and physical well-being. Experts say the average adult requires 7-8 hours of sleep each night, but it varies for each individual. When you don't have uninterrupted, peaceful, restorative sleep, it will affect your mood and productivity. This can lead to irritability, frustration and increased depression. When you don't get enough sleep, whatever is troubling you will seem to be worse and more impossible than it really is.

"Life goes on." "Time heals." "Tomorrow is another day." If you have not already, you will probably be offered these timeworn adages until they make you want to scream. These statements are bothersome because continuing to live is an affront to the memory of our lost loved one. Conversely, one should not try to "move on" until truly ready to. Brushing aside your feelings of sadness and pain will only perpetuate them. When should we start getting on with life? The answer is different for each one of us. Foremost, it is vital that we tackle the complex and troubling emotions suicide has left in us. Some survivors might come to a reasoned and acceptable understanding of their tragedy within a few months, but most will take a year to get through the toughest parts, and a year or two more to feel ready to live again. Refrain from making any significant life decisions in the first year, because you are likely to regret rash choices made in an hour of grief. However, life has a way of moving us forward, ready or not. New events and happenings occur; new faces enter our lives. Sometimes the mere arrival of these new developments only serves to remind us our loved one is not here to share in them; it might even feel as if you are "leaving them behind." You will never leave the memory of your loved one behind any more than you can take their physical being with you. With time and healing, you will be able to cherish fond memories of them while celebrating their life as you continue to live yours.

Every emotional response common to grief is intensified and complicated to almost unbearable dimensions following suicide. We are in dread of extreme societal points of view and religious biases. We fear for our surviving children. We become possessed with guilt and unrealistic acceptance of responsibility. My own guilt was so intense, I accepted the judgment that my son's suicide meant there was something wrong with me, and not him. At the same instant we feel a colossal sense of rejection, ineptitude, personal failure and anger ... anger at a higher power, at ourselves, occasionally at other family members and, perhaps most disturbing of all, at our dead child.

Gratitude is said to be the ideal mental attitude. That is because a grateful person is a happy person. People who are happy count their blessings. They focus on what they have rather than on what they don't have or on what is wrong in their lives. Grieving people tend to focus on what is wrong and how bad they feel, making it difficult for them to experience the joy of gratitude. After losing a child to suicide, the idea of feeling grateful about anything sounds ludicrous, and telling someone who is grieving and depressed to be thankful for all they have will only make them feel worse. Guilt about being depressed and sad only intensifies grief. Instead, it's better for a grieving person to practice being aware of things that are going right in their lives, no matter how great or small. Recognizing simple, everyday blessings is more helpful than looking at the big picture. For example, you can be thankful for your home and family; however, learning to recognize, appreciate and enjoy a loving hug, help with a chore, a new furnishing for the home, ability to pay a bill, and so forth can help to develop a daily habit of gratitude. A helpful way to establish this new habit is to write down at least one thing that was a blessing every day. It can be anything from a good day to a new insight, a phone call you received, a good deal you got shopping, and so forth. This exercise helps to train the mind to recognize and acknowledge the good things. As it is practiced, it comes more naturally, and it becomes a habit or way of life.

WHEN TO SEEK HELP

There are some symptoms that indicate you have had all the stress you can handle alone. The presence of any of these symptoms says it is time to call in professional help. Remember: there is no shame in seeking help. The only shame would be to require help and not get it.

Persistent thoughts of self-destruction. The key word is persistent. It is not unusual to have suicidal thoughts while experiencing grief, but they should pass quickly. If you begin thinking of a specific method and occasion for taking your life, seek help. "I will live" is a necessary decision for healthy grief.

Failure to provide for basic needs. If you find yourself changing your patterns of activity and avoiding friends and family, it is time to seek help. Interaction with other people is essential to healthy grief. Equally important is paying attention to your physical needs, including nutrition, fluids, exercise, rest, and personal hygiene. If you are failing to take care of these fundamental needs, it is time to seek help.

Persistence of one particular reaction to grief. Depression that immobilizes you for weeks is a sign that professional help is needed; so is continued denial of the reality of your loss, or finding yourself still without feelings months later. Help is needed when any normal grief reactions persist.

Substance abuse. This means everything from using tranquilizers or sleeping pills for too long, to engaging in alcohol or drug abuse. It also includes eating too much, too little, or surviving on junk food.

Mental illness. Persistent feelings of anxiety, hallucinations, or a collapse of body functions indicates emotional breakdown. A good rule of thumb: Any time you are unable to function normally, seek professional help. There is no shame in seeking help. The only shame would be to need help and not get it.

VIEWING THE BODY

You may have to choose whether to view the body of the deceased before or at the funeral, or whether to view the body at all. If you prefer, you can choose a private family viewing before anyone else arrives, to allow time to get over the initial shock and be more in control in public. There is only one fixed rule about viewing the body: Do whatever you feel like doing or not doing. There is no right or wrong way to do it. Many people find that viewing the body before the service helps them comprehend the reality of the death. Seeing the body of your loved one in a casket makes it difficult to run and hide from the loss. It also can bring a sense of comfort if you were not there when your loved one died, or if that person had suffered a lingering, debilitating illness and now appears at peace. It isn't wrong to touch the body. Choosing not to view the body is also okay. You may need to remember the person as you last saw him or her. It may be that the circumstances surrounding the death make it impossible or undesirable for you to view the body. If you have heart problems or high blood pressure, it may be preferable for you to deal with the loss more slowly. Whatever you choose is perfectly okay as long as it is not a way of denying the death. If you can't decide what to do and are in good physical health, I suggest you view the body in private, then decide what you want to do at the funeral.

FUNERAL PLANNING

A funeral typically takes place three to five days after a death. However, delays may occur because of the cause of death, the distance family members have to travel, weather, and availability of a facility or someone to officiate. Your time for the next few days will be consumed with decision-making. If you are responsible for making arrangements, you'll have to do a number of things. Choose a mortuary. Make decisions about the date and time of the funeral. Decide whether the casket will be open or closed. Decide whether to have a memorial service without the body present. Make arrangements for the body to be buried in an earthen grave or aboveground crypt. Choose embalming or cremation. If cremation is chosen, decide if the cremains are to be buried, placed in a niche, or scattered. Select someone to officiate at the funeral. In most cases that will be a priest, rabbi, or minister. Sometimes, it is a friend or public official. Make seemingly endless phone calls, each of which is just as hard to make as the one before it. Locate any insurance papers, birth certificates, and military records. In some circumstances, decide if there is to be an autopsy. Arrange to obtain copies of the death certificate.

You probably will not want to do any of this, but it must be done. You might find all the activity to be an unexpected benefit. Friends of the deceased or relatives who have no demands made upon them often find it is harder to cope in the first few days than do friends or family who have assumed responsibility for making the arrangements. For many people, making funeral arrangements and doing the other necessary tasks gives structure to an unstructured time and provides some clarity at a time when everything else seems unreal.

As painful as a funeral is, I would advise that you don't take sedatives, drugs, or alcohol before the funeral. The service is intended to help you more than it is to do anything for the deceased. To get the most help from the funeral, you need to be as aware as possible of what is happening. Be in touch with your feelings. Express your grief. The funeral may be the first time the death becomes real for you. As painful as this moment is, undergoing the reality of your loss at the funeral can be quite important to you a few weeks or months down the road, because the only way out of grief is through it.

Also remember that neither you nor anyone in your family needs to be strong for each other or for friends and community at this time. It is not your job to show how well you can care for everyone else.

Before the funeral at some point, take time to be alone. Dedicate at least an hour to this important task. Say out loud to yourself: "_____ is dead; he or she is dead." Don't say gone or passed away or passed on. Use the word dead. You need to hear yourself say it.

AFTER THE FUNERAL

For some days following the death of a loved one, you will be surrounded by caring family members and friends. But all too soon the day comes when family members must return to their own lives, and friends seem tired of coping with your grief. They will rally to your side and be ready to listen to your complaints and comfort your tears for a few days. Then they will go back to their own lives and expect you to get on with yours.

One day you are the center of attention, and it seems everybody cares about you and shares your loss. You wake up the next day, and everybody is gone. You are more alone than you have ever been in your entire life. It becomes very quiet, and the silence is deafening. Being with people through the funeral is good. But it is after the funeral that the real work of grief recovery begins, and lasts for a long time. Three years or more is not unreasonable or abnormal.

After any major loss, you may have a difficult time reaching out for help. People will tell you to call them whenever you need them. At the moment you need them the most, the thought of calling others may never cross your mind! You will feel lonely and confused. You will wish somebody would come along to do something without your having to ask. Most of the time, no one will come. It doesn't mean no one cares. It simply reflects the truth that not many people understand loss and grief.

SUICIDE WARNING SIGNS

Suicide doesn't discriminate based on age, gender, religion or race. The wealthy and the poor are vulnerable. Since Jeff died, I have come to understand that suicide is a serious public health issue. According to the National Institute of Mental Health, around 30,000 people die by suicide every year in the United States. More people die by suicide every year than by homicide.

Suicide is not a rational reaction to stress; it is a sign of extreme distress, and it is not a harmless bid for attention (as some people believe). Suicide remains one of the top three leading causes of death for young people ages 15 to 24.

The risk for suicidal behavior has also been found to be associated with changes in the brain's neurotransmitter serotonin. Lower levels of serotonin have been found in the brains of people with a history of suicide attempts. Although many people show these risk factors, they don't always attempt suicide.

According to the American Foundation for Suicide Prevention, some suicides occur without any warning signs, but a majority of people who are suicidal do give warnings. You can prevent the suicide of loved ones by learning to recognize the signs of someone at risk, taking those signs seriously, and knowing how to respond to them.

Observable signs of severe depression

- Unrelenting low mood

- Pessimism

- Hopelessness

- Desperation

- Anxiety, emotional pain and emotional tension

- Withdrawal

- Sleep problems

- Increased alcohol and/or other drug use

- Recent impulsiveness and taking unnecessary risks

- Threatening suicide or expressing a strong wish to die

Making a plan

- Giving away prized possessions

- Sudden or impulsive procurement of a firearm

- Obtaining other means of killing oneself such as poisons or medications

- Unexpected rage or anger

PREVENTION

The emotional crises that usually precede suicide are often recognizable and treatable. Although most depressed people are not suicidal, most suicidal people are depressed. Serious depression can be manifested in obvious sadness, but often it is expressed as a loss of enjoyment in, or withdrawal from, activities that had once been entertaining. Suicide can be prevented through early identification and treatment of depression and other psychiatric illnesses.

Simply by knowing what the risk factors for suicide are, and who is at risk, can help reduce the risk of suicide. I will never know if I would have been able to prevent my son's death. I wish I had known he was at risk, and then maybe I could have gotten him the help he needed, but would not ask for. The cruelty of suicide is not knowing what they were thinking when they decided to end their very existence.

According to the Centers for Disease Control and Prevention, there were 38,364 suicide deaths reported in 2010. This places suicide as the tenth-leading cause of death in America. The national suicide rate increased 3.9 percent over 2009 to total approximately 12.4 suicides per 100,000 people. Tragically, the rate of suicide has been increasing since 2000. We are currently experiencing the highest rate of suicide in 15 years.

Effective suicide prevention is based on sound research. Programs that work take into account people's risk factors and promote interventions that are relevant to particular groups of people. For example, research has shown that mental disorders and substance abuse are risk factors for suicide. Therefore, many programs focus on treating these disorders and addressing suicide risk specifically.

At this time, there is only one medication, clozapine, approved by the FDA for suicide risk reduction in patients with schizophrenia. There is some evidence from retrospective studies that the atypical antipsychotics, especially clozapine, reduced death by suicide in schizophrenics treated with these medications compared to similar patients not treated with these medications. In addition, there is a long-term follow-up study of mood disorder patients that shows that treatment with antidepressants, atypical antipsychotics and lithium reduced death by suicide, again compared to those who did not receive these treatments. There are meta-analyses of small lithium studies that show suicide is reduced in those patients with either bipolar disorder or serious depression taking lithium, but there are other studies that don't support that claim. So the lithium statistics for suicide risk reduction are still controversial.

There are two proven psychotherapies for treating those who attempt suicide: cognitive behavior therapy (CBT) for suicide attempters, and dialectical behavioral therapy (DBT) for patients with borderline personality disorder and recurrent suicidal ideation and behaviors. Clearly these short-term interactive therapies make a difference. The goal now is to convey evidence-based treatments into community-based settings. There are many small studies of various interventions, including encouraging short-term therapies that involve the family that show repeat suicide attempts are reduced under the treatment condition being tested. These need to be replicated and tested in a controlled way before they can be adopted for the greater population. A therapist trained in DBT helps a person recognize when his or her feelings or actions are disruptive or unhealthy, and teaches the skills needed to deal with upsetting situations better.

Still other research has found that many older adults and women who die by suicide saw their primary care providers in the year before their death. Training doctors to recognize signs that a person may be considering suicide may help prevent even more suicides. Research shows that teaching health care professionals to recognize and treat depression is an effective way to reduce suicide rates. If the depression is mild, the doctor may begin with psychotherapy alone, and add medication later if the symptoms don't improve.

Many medications are available to treat depression, the most common of which are antidepressants. The FDA currently approves about 22 medications. Since there is no accurate test to match a person's symptoms and complaints with the right medication, there is no way to know which medication will work best for a particular person. The person who may be depressed should discuss with their doctor the medication choice and how to take it as well as the possible side effects. The doctor needs to be told about all the other prescription medications the person is taking as well as nonprescription medications, vitamins and supplements, and their daily alcohol intake. Alcohol intake should be minimal while taking an antidepressant or any psychotropic medication. Sometimes there is the need to try a few different medications before finding the one that gives the best result with minimal side effects. When the optimal dose with the best medication is achieved, the antidepressant may take from 4–12 weeks to achieve maximum benefit, but it is possible for one or two symptoms to improve in the first few weeks.

When antidepressants are started, or when doses are increased, a few patients, especially children, adolescents and young adults, may experience increased anxiety, agitation, restlessness, irritability or anger, which may lead to suicidal thoughts or attempts. The doctor should outline these risks and warning signs before the treatment begins. If the patient or the family sees this developing, they should immediately call the doctor. The doctor will either add a medication to lessen the symptoms, reduce the dose, or change the medication. Initially, the doctor may also prescribe the medications in small amounts to minimize the results of any impulsive or suicidal behavior.

If the person is not feeling better after 12 weeks on the medication, the doctor may add an additional antidepressant, another drug, switch to a different antidepressant, or add psychotherapy if it has not already been instigated.

The doctor may ask the patient to take a depression rating scale so that both the patient and the doctor can determine whether things are improving. The treatment should be continued until the patient is no longer experiencing symptoms. Even after that is achieved, the doctor will typically recommend continuing the treatment for another 9–12 months. If the person is not feeling better after six months, it is wise to seek a second opinion.

Beyond medicines, specific types of psychotherapies have been proven effective for treating depression. These are usually short-term, lasting from 12–16 weeks, and they are formalized and interactive. Sessions may take place one to two times a week, with a professional who has been specifically trained and certified in the treatment they are using.

The most common types of psychotherapy for depression are cognitive behavior therapy (CBT), interpersonal therapy (IPT), behavioral activation (BH), and the cognitive behavioral analysis system of psychotherapy (CBASP). There is clear evidence from research studies that combining antidepressants with any one of these psychotherapies is the best treatment for "chronic" depression (defined as having had a depressive illness for two years or more). Supportive psychotherapy for depression is less well defined. The therapist may be a physician, psychiatrist, psychologist, social worker, psychiatric nurse or a psychotherapist or counselor.

Unfortunately, the nature of depressive illness is that, even after it is successfully treated, it often recurs. Antidepressants and some of the therapies noted above can prevent or reduce the frequency of these recurrences. Continuing treatment for a longer term, or coming back to treatment, can help. The patient and the doctor should discuss the best way to approach the long-term treatment of the illness.

Marian Betz, M.D., M.P.H., an assistant professor in the Department of Emergency Medicine at the University of Colorado in Denver, is working to identify the attitudes and behaviors of emergency department (ED) doctors and nurses towards asking about access to firearms and other lethal means. More than half of suicides are by firearms, and limiting access to lethal means has been proven around the world to decrease suicides. ED staff can play a critical role in suicide prevention.

The University of Colorado is one of eight centers collaborating in ED-SAFE, a NIMH-funded study to learn how emergency departments across the nation can improve their suicide assessments and interventions. Dr. Betz is using her AFSP Young Investigator Grant to study how ED personnel interact with suicidal patients with regard to the availability of guns and gun safety.

Her findings have been published in the April 2013 issue of *Depression and Anxiety*.

After surveying 631 ED physicians and nurses, she found that 49% of doctors and 72% of nurses reported that they "hardly ever" personally counsel patients or families to temporarily remove or lock up guns at home. She also found that 44% of doctors and 67% of nurses believed that most or all people who die by suicide by gun would find another way to kill themselves if the gun was not available to them. Less than half of the staff considered suicide as preventable.

These findings demonstrate the importance of asking about access to lethal means and discussing ways to keep the suicidal person safe. These researchers are currently testing a program that teaches ED staff about suicide and how to screen for suicide risk, and how to conduct brief interventions, including training about access to lethal means.

Hungary had one of the highest rates of suicide in the world when AFSP funded a study to teach general practitioners how to identify and treat depressed patients to lower suicide rates. This study was aimed at improving physicians' skills at assessing depression and suicidal ideation and behavior in patients. In one region, physicians received a four-session education program about depression and its treatment as well as access to mental health consultation. A second region with comparable suicide rates did not receive the training. Suicide rates in the five years before the program (1996–2000) were compared with rates during the five years after the program (2001–2005). Suicide rates decreased in the intervention region and the control region as well as the county and the country as a whole over the five years, with greater decreases in the region that received the education program. Along with reduced suicide rates, they found that, in the intervention region, there were increases in antidepressant prescription rates. This study demonstrates that educating the medical community about depression and its treatment reduces suicide rates.

Can we prevent suicide by reducing access to lethal methods? Dr. David Gunnell from the University of Bristol has demonstrated that the answer is "yes." He investigated the impact of placing preventive barriers on the Clifton Suspension Bridge in Bristol, England—a site from which suicide by jumping frequently occurred and was typically fatal. His study covered ten years: five before the barriers were constructed and five after. He found that during the five years before the barriers were put in place, those who jumped tended to be less likely to have engaged in prior self-harm and less likely to have received psychiatric services, suggesting that these acts were more impulsive. In the five years after the construction of the barriers, the number of deaths was cut in half, and most of the reduction was seen in males. After the barriers were put in place, the few who died tended to have more chronic problems and their deaths were not seen as impulsive acts. There was no increase of deaths by jumping at other bridges in the area during the five years after the barriers were installed. Interviews with the bridge staff indicated that although they initially opposed the barriers and thought they would not be effective, they found that it helped them to "buy time" and intervene. They noted that a camera for bridge staff to monitor activity on the bridge was essential. For architectural reasons, the barriers were not placed on the buttress walls at either end of the bridge. In view of the continued, although much reduced, suicides at this site, further work to improve the safety of the site is underway. Dr. Gunnell has gone on to study other effects of limiting access to lethal means. While not a cure for suicide, this study shows that limiting bridge access can reduce suicide by "buying time" for assistance through a suicide crisis.

As part of an AFSP grant, Jeff Bridge, Ph.D., and his colleagues studied decision-making in teenagers who have made a suicide attempt. He looked at how teens control their thoughts and behaviors, their levels of aggression, and their tolerance for being provoked or frustrated. He compared the levels of impulsivity, aggression, and impulsive aggression in suicide attempters and similar youth who were in the same treatment programs and had not made a suicide attempt. The results were published in the April 2012 issue of the *American Journal of Child & Adolescent Psychiatry*. The study included 40 adolescents aged 13 to 18 who had recently made a suicide attempt, and 40 matched adolescents who had never made a suicide attempt. Dr. Bridge collected data on the Iowa Gambling Task (IGT), a computerized gambling task that provides an evaluation of decision-making. Participants also filled out questionnaires and were interviewed about their impulsiveness, aggression and their past and present psychiatric treatment. Adolescents who had attempted suicide were less likely to learn how to maximize decision-making to earn the most money compared to the other psychiatrically ill adolescents. Group differences in mood disorders, psychiatric medications, impulsivity and hostility did not account for their poor choices. They found no relationship between the poor decision-making performance and any characteristics of the attempt such as time since last suicide attempt, number of previous attempts, intent to die, or medical consequences of the attempt. Overall, the results support other research that suggests inflexible decision-making may play a role in increasing risk for suicidal attempts. Dr. Bridge has used data from his study to secure a five-year, $2.1 million research grant from the National Institute of Mental Health (NIMH) titled "Impulsive Aggression, Neurocognition, and Suicidal Behavior in Depressed Youth" that will start in July 2012. This work has the potential to help with the development of practical suicide risk evaluation tools, treatments and preventive interventions to reduce adolescent suicidal behavior. An added value from Dr. Bridge's AFSP grant was that Neel Koyawala, a senior at a local Columbus, Ohio high school, used data from Dr. Bridge's AFSP grant to conduct an independent, mentored research project examining the relationship between sleep problems and adolescent suicidal behavior. According to

Dr. Bridge, Neel's results showed that self-reported sleep problems were associated with adolescent suicidal behavior, even after taking into account current antidepressant medication use, depression, and being bullied. Neel submitted his study to the Young Epidemiology Scholars Program National Competition. In April 2011, he presented the findings in Washington, D.C. and finished in the top 12 (of 562) applicants, earning him a $15,000 scholarship. (Neel is currently attending the University of Pennsylvania where he plans to study biochemistry. Jeff Bridge, Ph.D., is an epidemiologist at the Center for Innovation in Pediatric Practice at Columbus Children's Research Institute and an Associate Professor of Pediatrics at the Ohio State University College of Medicine. He conducted this research with a Young Investigator Grant from AFSP.)

Madelyn Gould, Ph.D., M.P.H., used her AFSP Standard Research Grant to study the relationship between bullying and suicide in high school students and dispel the media portrayal of bullying as a singular cause of suicide. Dr. Gould's findings indicate that experiencing bullying in combination with other risk factors such as past suicidal ideation or attempts, depression and substance use raises the risk for suicidal behavior. Bullying, by itself, doesn't necessarily lead to increased suicidal behavior. This is one of the first studies to focus on bullying and suicidal behavior using a longitudinal, rather than cross-sectional, approach. The investigators surveyed students in the ninth through twelfth grades from six New York State high schools to determine both their risk for suicidal behavior and their exposure to bullying. Risk for suicidal behavior was defined as a past or recent suicidal ideation or attempt, at least moderate current depression and/or problems caused by substance use. The cohort of students was divided into four groups: 1) not at risk for suicidal behavior and not bullied; 2) "at-risk" and not bullied; 3) not at risk and bullied, and 4) "at-risk" and bullied and/ or bullying others. The "at-risk" groups were followed-up two years later, and the "bully only" group was assessed four years later. Dr. Gould found that bullying was only associated with later suicidal ideation or attempts for "at-risk" students. Those who were bullied without the other risk factors had increased levels of depression over time, but overall they had fewer psychiatric problems than did those students who were already at risk for suicidal behavior regardless of bullying. Her findings indicate that the media focus on the relationship of bullying and suicide may be ignoring a stronger underlying issue. She suggests that bullying should be a factor in screening for suicide risk, but rather than placing the blame for suicidal ideation and behavior solely on bullies, we can begin to see bullying as a critical factor adding to pre-existing risk factors such as depression, anxiety and substance use problems. Bullying has a negative affect all students. (Madelyn Gould, Ph.D., M.P.H., is a Professor of Clinical Epidemiology in Psychiatry at Columbia University, College of Physicians and Surgeons, and a Research Scientist at the New York State Psychiatric Institute.)

Mark Kaplan, M.P.H, Dr.P.H., an AFSP Distinguished Investigator, and colleagues have conducted a general population study of suicide antecedents among women and men with a history of U.S. military service. Unlike most veteran suicide studies that are conducted within the Veterans Administration, Dr. Kaplan's study used the National Violent Death Reporting System (NVDRS), a state-based surveillance system that gathers information from death certificates, police reports, and coroner or medical examiner reports to provide detailed information about individuals who die by a violent death. This database, available in 16 states at the time of the study, provides valuable information about different risks for suicide related to military status, age, gender, recent stressors and many other factors. The investigators found that veterans were at a much higher risk for suicide than non-veterans; especially women, who had nearly triple the rate of suicide relative to women who never served in the military. Veterans, especially older veterans, were also more likely to die by firearms. Dr. Kaplan and colleagues found notable differences between the risk profiles of individuals who died by firearms and those who died by other means. Individuals who died by firearms were more likely to have experienced a stressful life event during the two weeks before death. Individuals who died by other means were more likely to have a diagnosis of mental illness and a previous suicide attempt. Dr. Kaplan and colleagues also investigated the relationship between age and suicide among male veterans and found that mental illness, substance abuse, and financial and relationship problems were more common in younger veterans. Nearly one-third of the youngest veterans had a Blood Alcohol Concentration (BAC) greater than or equal to .08 based on toxicological data, regardless of whether they had a longstanding alcohol abuse problem. By contrast, fewer than 10% of veterans over age 65 were found to have BACs high enough to indicate intoxication at the time of death, and older men were more likely to have health problems. Dr. Kaplan received a large grant from the National Institute on Alcohol Abuse and Alcoholism (NIAAA) based on the findings of this study. AFSP strongly supports the development of the NVDRS, in all states in the U.S.

Stephanie Kasen, Ph.D., received an AFSP Standard Research Grant to investigate the development of impulsivity, feelings of capability and suicide attempts from ages 10-25. Using a unique longitudinal database of 766 children and their mothers assessed three times across ten years, Dr. Kasen examined the trajectories of 68 youth who reported a suicide attempt (8.8% of the sample) since the initial assessment and compared them with 702 youth who reported they had not made a suicide attempt after the initial assessment. The participants were age 13.7 at baseline, 16.1 at three years and 22.0 at ten years. Her findings were published in the journal *Suicide and Life Threatening Behavior* in April 2011. Impulsivity was measured by a questionnaire assessing behavioral control, respect for social limits, and ease of being provoked and maladaptive or inappropriate responses. Capability, or a sense of being capable, was measured by a questionnaire that reflected attributes related to self-esteem and a sense of mastery. She found that all youth had declining impulsivity over time but those who had made a suicide attempt reported greater impulsivity at all time-points and declined more slowly. At age 17, those with attempts had impulsivity levels six times greater than those who had not attempted. In contrast, a sense of capability increased over time for all participants but those who had made attempts had lower levels of capability at each time point and never reached the levels that those who had not attempted reached. Their rate of increasing capability was slower than non-attempters. Maternal risk (defined as having had a mother who had a history of a Major Depressive Disorder or a suicide attempt) and a history of having experienced physical or sexual abuse were related to impulsivity but not capability. Dr. Kasen's study afforded the opportunity to examine the relationships among impulsivity, sense of capability and suicide attempts over the developmental period of adolescence. It shows that while some degree of increased impulsivity in the early teens is common, excessive impulsivity or limited decline of impulsivity is not typical and may relate to attempt risk. Simultaneously, youth develop an increased sense of competence over time and feeling less effective may indicate increased risk for a suicide attempt, especially in the context of increased impulsivity. This affords developing interventions that assist in improving socially appropriate behavior and increasing a sense of personal ability to reduce the risk for suicide attempts in adolescents. (Dr. Kasen is a research scientist in the Division of Epidemiology at New York State Psychiatric Institute, and Associate Clinical Professor of Medical Psychology in Psychiatry, College of Physicians and Surgeons, Columbia University.)

If you know someone who is considering suicide, don't leave him or her alone. Try to get your loved one to seek immediate help from his or her doctor or the nearest hospital emergency room, or call 911. Remove any access he or she may have to firearms or other possible tools for suicide, including medications.

If you are in crisis, call the toll-free National Suicide Prevention Lifeline at 1-800-273-TALK (8255), available 24 hours a day, 7 days a week. The service is available to anyone. All calls are confidential.

CORPSMAN'S OATH

I solemnly pledge myself before God and these
witnesses to practice faithfully all of my duties as a
member of the hospital corps.

I hold the care of the sick and injured to be a sacred trust
and will assist the medical officer with loyalty and
honesty.

I will not knowingly permit harm to come to any
patient.

I will not partake of nor administer any unauthorized
medication.

I will hold all personal matters pertaining to the private
lives of patients in strict confidence.

I dedicate my heart, mind, and strength to the work
before me. I shall do all within my power to show in
myself an example of all that is honorable and good
throughout my naval career.

A LETTER TO MY SON

Saying good-bye is never easy. Saying good-bye to a deceased loved one hurts beyond words. However, before you can open new doors for your life, you have to close the doors that now lead to the past. It doesn't mean forgetting the person or memories any more than you forget your friends when they go home after a meal at your home.

To say good-bye acknowledges you will not share life with a person anymore, other than in memory. The person is forever frozen in time for you. They will get no older than the day they died. You will. Writing this letter is an act of releasing a part of your life that will always remain important to you in memory, but which you must now leave behind. It is essential to say good-bye to those you will not see again in this life.

Because you can't say good-bye in person to the one who has died, an alternative is to write them a letter. If you are like nearly all people who have done this, it will be the most difficult letter you have ever written. It helps to remember that this is also one of the most important letters you will ever write. This is the letter I wrote to my son Jeff.

Jeff,

I miss you so very much, I can't believe you're really gone. I hear your voice, I see your face, and I feel your presence. We have conversations every day. I often wonder if you're really here, or I'm just imagining that you are.

I don't understand why you felt you had to leave. I would have done anything to help you, to make you happy, to make you want to stay. I have tried to accept you were not capable of asking for help, but it doesn't make it hurt any less.

I have not forgotten you. I think about you all the time. You were always so giving of yourself, and you took so much joy in giving gifts, just like your mom. I miss your smile and your laugh. I loved seeing you grow into a young man; you made me feel like a great Dad.

I will always love you. I wish you were still here with me. There is nothing that can replace you. One day I hope to think of you as someone who lived, not someone who died.

Goodbye my son, I will always be grateful for the brief time I had you in my life.

FORGIVENESS

Relationships can cause great joy as well as terrible pain. Hurtful words, broken promises, disrespect, abusive behavior and especially suicide can all leave a person deeply wounded. If the underlying hurt or offense is not processed and resolved, it leads to unforgiveness. Prolonged unforgiveness leads to bitterness and depression. When this occurs, letting go of resentment becomes necessary to continue the healing process.

Resolution with the person who caused the pain is not possible when they are deceased. So resolution has to occur in the heart of the person that was hurt. Forgiveness doesn't justify the wrong actions of another or make them right. It doesn't excuse the wrong done. Forgiveness releases the person who was hurt from the chains of pain and anger that keep them bound. Forgiveness begins when you have a willingness to forgive. You might not feel you are able to forgive, but being willing is the first step. Feelings eventually catch up to decisions. Sometimes forgiveness is accomplished in layers, and it may be necessary to forgive each time a memory or feeling emerges. Working through each layer helps to bring you closer to experiencing the freedom that forgiveness brings, whether it is you that you need to forgive or someone that has hurt you.

RESOURCES

In 1999, Senator Harry Reid introduced a resolution to the United States Senate, which eventually led to the creation of a National Survivors of Suicide Day. Reid proposed the designation after his own father died by suicide. This national event later evolved into an international event observed by many countries throughout the world.

The Saturday before Thanksgiving is now designated International Survivors of Suicide Day and on this most memorable day friends and family of those who have completed suicide join for healing and comfort. The American Foundation for Suicide Prevention (AFSP) currently sponsors the American day. Every year, survivors of suicide loss meet in locations around the world to feel a sense of community, to promote healing, and to connect with others that have had similar experiences. Each location welcomes survivors of suicide loss, providing a safe and healing space where everyone can comfortably participate in a way that is meaningful to them.

I attended the conference for the first time on November 17, 2012. Not since Jeff's funeral had I felt such a sense of togetherness and support. Having so many people connected by the same kind of loss made my sadness and despair feel so much more bearable. In all I would guess there were around 250 attendees. We watched a video depicting other survivors discussing their experience with loss, grieving and recovery. Following the video we broke into three distinct groups. My group focused on grief recovery. We formed a large circle, and then began sharing our experiences with one another. This was such a powerful experience because there were at least 75 people sharing a subject so near and dear to my heart. Telling my story, as well as listening to other stories with remarkable similarities to my own, is imperative to a survivor of suicide simply because suicide is perhaps the most complicated death of all to deal with. Following the breakout sessions, we all reconvened in the main area to begin the candle-lighting ceremony.

Placed on a table in front of the room were two tall candlesticks surrounded by hundreds of tea-light candles. The two taller candles were lit. The first candle representing the one we lost was blown out, the second candle symbolizing remembrance and our desire to heal was left burning. Then mourners were called upon to light the remaining candles in recognition of their beloved. When everyone finished lighting the smaller candles, we sat in a moment of silence, a silence more eloquent than any words could have ever been.

Survivor groups can help fill the void of isolation. Others will more than likely tire of talking about your loss long before you do. Talking through your feelings and fears is essential for recovery from your trauma. Unfortunately, while your closest supporters may be willing to listen and share with you for a few weeks or months, there's likely to come a time when their thoughts move on from the suicide while yours are still racing. This is why support groups are so helpful. Fellow survivors know what you are feeling in a way even your closest friends and family cannot. Your fellow group members will never grow tired of offering encouraging words and sympathetic ears.

There are many support groups available throughout the United States. The following is a list of some of the resources currently available.

- The American Association of Suicidology (AAS) is a membership organization for all those involved in suicide prevention and intervention, or touched by suicide. AAS is a leader in the advancement of scientific and programmatic efforts in suicide prevention through research, education and training, the development of standards and resources, and survivor support. Their purpose is to understand and prevent suicide.

(202) 237-2280
www.suicidology.org

- The Alliance of Hope for Suicide Survivors is a nonprofit that provides therapeutic support for people who have lost loved ones to suicide. Ronnie Walker, a licensed clinical mental health counselor who lost her stepson to suicide in 1995, founded the Alliance of Hope for Suicide Survivors in 2008.

(847) 868-3313
www.allianceofhope.org

- Friends For Survival, Inc. is a national nonprofit outreach organization open to those who have lost relatives or friends by suicide, and to professionals who work with those who have been touched by a suicide tragedy. Friends for Survival, organized by and for survivors, has been offering support since 1983. All staff and volunteers have been directly affected by a suicide death.

(916) 392-0664
www.friendsforsurvival.org

- HEARTBEAT is peer support offering empathy, encouragement and direction following the suicide of a loved one.

(719) 596-2527
www.heartbeatsurvivorsaftersuicide.org

- The American Foundation for Suicide Prevention (AFSP) is one of the nation's leading organizations bringing together people across communities and backgrounds to understand and prevent suicide, and to help lessen the pain it causes. Individuals, families, and communities who have been personally touched by suicide are the moving force behind everything they do.

(212) 363-3500
www.afsp.org

- The American Psychiatric Association, founded in 1844, is the world's largest psychiatric organization. It is a medical specialty society representing more than 33,000 psychiatric physicians from the United States and around the world. Its member physicians work together to ensure humane care and effective treatment for all persons with mental disorders, including intellectual disabilities and substance abuse disorders. APA is the voice and conscience of modern psychiatry.

- (888)-357-7924 and press 0

www.psych.org

- The American Psychological Association is the largest scientific and professional organization representing psychology in the United States. APA is the world's largest association of psychologists, with more than 134,000 researchers, educators, clinicians, consultants and students as its members. Their goal is to promote the creation, dissemination and application of psychological knowledge to benefit society and improve people's lives.

(800)-964-2000
www.apa.org

- The National Association of Social Workers (NASW) is the largest membership organization of professional social workers in the world, with 145,000 members. NASW works to improve the professional growth and development of its members, to create and maintain professional standards, and to promote healthy social policies.

www.naswdc.org

- Department of Veterans Affairs

www.mentalhealth.va.gov/gethelp.asp

- U.S. Substance and Mental Health Services Administration

www.store.samhsa.gov/mhlocator

- Depression & Bipolar Support Alliance

www.dbsalliance.org

- The Anxiety and Depression Association of America (ADAA) is the leader in education, training, and research for anxiety, depression, and stress related disorders.

www.adaa.org/findinghelp/treatment

Alabama

Birmingham: Crisis Center, Inc. 205-323-7782
Florence: Day-by-day 205-766-9161
Montgomery: Survivors of Suicide 334-270-4100

Alaska

Anchorage: Support Group for Suicide Survivors
907-272-3100
Fairbanks: Fairbanks Crisis Line 907-451-8600

Arizona

Tempe: Survivors of Suicide 602-784-1514
Yuma: Survivors of Suicide 520-783-1860

Arkansas

Little Rock: Survivors of Suicide, Arkansas Chapter
501-337-1930

California

Berkeley: Survivors of Suicide 510-889-1104
Burlingame: Survivors of Suicide 415-692-6662
Castro Valley: Survivors of Suicide 510-889-1104
Chico: Suicide Survivors Bereavement Support Group
916-891-2832
Davis: Friends and Families of Suicide Loss 916-756-7542
Fresno: Fresno Survivors of Suicide Loss 800-822-8448;
209-435-7669
Garden Grove: Survivors of Suicide 714-971-4032
Jackson: New Horizons 209-223-0793

Modesto: Survivors of Suicide 209-577-0615
Napa/Solano: Survivors of Suicide 707-252-6222
Pacific Grove: Loving Outreach for Survivors
408-375-6966
Redding: Suicide Survivors Support Group 916-225-5252
San Bernardino: Survivors of Suicide Support Group
909-792-4862
Sacramento: Friends for Survival 916-392-0664
San Diego: Survivors of Suicide 619-482-0297
San Francisco: Self Help Grief Group 415-750-5355
San Luis Obispo: Suicide Survivors Group 805-544-2266
Santa Barbara: Suicide Survivors 805-965-5555
Santa Rosa: Survivors of Suicide 707-542-5045
Upland: Hope After Suicide 909-982-7534
Vacaville: Bay Area Survivors of Suicide 707-452-8520
Walnut Creek: Survivors of Suicide 510-944-0645

Colorado

Arvada: Heartbeat 303-424-4094
Boulder: Heartbeat 303-444-3496
Colorado Springs: Heartbeat 719-596-2575
Denver: Heartbeat 303-934-8464
Denver: Parents of Suicides 303-322-7450
Denver: Survivors Group 303-766-3328
Florence: Heartbeat 719-269-2140
Ft Collins: Suicide Resource Center 970-635-9301
Grand Junction: Heartbeat 970-243-2467
Greeley: Suicide Education and Support Services
970-353-0639
Littleton: Heartbeat 303-794-3564
Pueblo: Heartbeat 719-564-6642
Connecticut
Hartford: Safe Place/The Samaritans of the Capital
Region 203-232-2121

Middletown: Survivors of Suicide 203-343-5814;
203-347-4003
Southbury: Survivors of Suicide 203-264-5613
Wethersfield: Suicide Bereavement 203-563-3035

Delaware

Millsboro: Survivors of Suicide 800-287-6423
Wilmington: Survivors of Suicide 302-656-8308

Florida

Altamonte Springs: Survivors of Suicide Support Group
407-869-9617
Boca Raton: Suicide Survivors Support Group
407-394-7979
Bradenton: Hospice of SW Florida 941-739-8940
Cape Coral: Survivors of Suicide 941-945-0338
Daytona Beach: Assure 904-252-5785; 904-756-3198
Ft. Lauderdale: Survivors of Suicide 305-467-6333
Jacksonville: Self Help Support Group 904-721-4282
Lauderhill: Suicide Survivors Support Group
954-968-6795
Miami: Suicide Survivors Support Group 305-653-1023
Palm Beach: The Courage to Survive 407-747-3165
Pensacola: Survivors of Suicide 904-438-9879
Pinellas Park: Survivors and Victims, United
813-791-3131
Rockledge: Crisis Services of Brevard, Inc. 407-631-8944

Georgia

Albany: Suicide Survivors 912-883-1281

Atlanta: Bereavement Support Group 404-505-7703; 404-758-1329

Atlanta: Survivors of Suicide, Sandy Springs Chapter 404-256-9797

Douglas County: Survivors of Suicide 770-432-1621

Henry County: Survivors of Suicide 770-914-0626

Lawrenceville: Survivors of Suicide 404-256-9797

Marietta: Survivors of Suicide, East Cobb Chapter 770-998-8819

Riverdale: Survivors of Suicide, Riverdale Chapter 770-998-8819

Roswell: Survivors of Suicide 770-993-6218

Hawaii

Honolulu: Survivors of Suicide 808-521-4555

Idaho

Boise: Survivors of Suicide 208-338-1017; 208-345-2350

Idaho Falls: Survivors of Suicide 208-522-0033

Illinois

Aurora: Survivors of Suicide 708-897-5522

Chicago: LOSS: Loving Outreach to Survivors of Suicide 312-655-7283

Decatur: Listening, Sharing, Caring (LSC) 217-767-2268

Edgemont: Survivors of Suicide 618-397-0963

Oak Brook: Compassionate Friends 708-990-0010

Peoria: Survivors of Suicide 309-693-5281; 309-697-3342

Wood River: The C.O.-H.E.A.R.T.S. 618-251-4073

Indiana

Bloomington: SOS/Heartbeat 812-334-3801
Columbus: Survivors of Suicide 812-546-5820
Elkhart: Survivors of Suicide 219-295-8156
Ft. Wayne: We the Living 219-422-6402; 219-432-6293
Lafayette: Survivors of Suicide Support Group
317-742-0460

Iowa

Cedar Falls: Suicide Grief Support Group 319-277-5369
Cedar Rapids: Suicide Survivors Group 319-362-2174
Iowa City: Ray of Hope 319-337-9890

Kansas

Topeka: Survivors of Suicide 913-267-4547

Kentucky

Louisville: Survivors of Suicide 502-589-4313
Middlesboro: Survivors of Suicide 606-248-1678
Owensboro: Survivors of Suicide 502-926-7565

Louisiana

Baton Rouge: Survivors of Suicide 504-924-1431;
504-924-3900
Monroe: Support After Suicide 318-323-9479
New Orleans: Coping with Suicide 504-834-1354

Maine

Portland: Survivors of Suicide 207-871-4226

Rumford: Survivors of Suicide 207-364-2651

Maryland

Baltimore: SEASONS: Suicide Bereavement 410-882-2937
Bethesda: SEASONS: Suicide Bereavement 301-460-4677
Crofton: Growing Through Grief 410-721-0899
Westminster: SEASONS: Suicide Bereavement
410-876-1047

Massachusetts

Andover: Safe Place/The Samaritans of Merrimack
Valley 508-688-6607
Boston: Safe Place/The Samaritans of Boston
617-536-2460
Fall River: Safe Place 508-673-3777
Falmouth: Safe Place/The Samaritans of Cape Cod
508-548-8900
Framingham: Safe Place/The Samaritans of Suburban
West 508-875-4500
West Springfield: Survivors of Suicide 413-734-9139

Michigan

Adrian: Survivors of Suicide 517-263-7882
Cadillac: Survivors of Suicide 616-826-3865
Detroit: Survivors of Suicide 313-224-7000
East Lansing: Survivors of Suicide 517-626-6317
Flint: Survivors of Suicide 810-232-9950
Grand Rapids: West Michigan Survivors of Suicide
616-281-2058
Jackson: Survivors of Suicide 517-783-2648
Kalamazoo: Survivors of Suicide 616-381-4357

Lansing: Survivors of Suicide 517-339-1529
Ludington: West Shore Survivors of Suicide
616-845-6854
Marquette: Survivors of Suicide 906-228-3040
Port Huron: Survivors of Suicide 810-794-4982
Saginaw: Survivors of Suicide 517-781-0410
Spring Lake: West Michigan Survivors of Suicide
616-874-6439
Troy: Survivors of Suicide 810-680-0796
Warren: Survivors of Suicide 810-307-9100

Minnesota

Duluth: Suicide Survivors Support Group 218-726-4402
Minneapolis: SAVE 612-946-7998
St. Paul: Survivors of Suicide 612-776-1565
Willmar: Support Group for Survivors of Suicide
612-235-5411

Mississippi

Jackson: Survivors of Suicide 601-360-0814

Missouri

Springfield: Survivors of Suicide Group 417-865-5943
St. Louis: Survivors of Suicide Support Group
314-647-3100

Montana

Missoula: Surviving Friends 406-543-6132

Nebraska

Hastings: Heartbeat 402-463-7804
Lincoln: Ray of Hope Survivors of Suicide 402-488-3827
Omaha: Survivors of Suicide Omaha 402-558-4616

Nevada

Reno: Survivors of Suicide 702-323-4533

New Hampshire

Derry: Coping with a Loved One's Suicide 603-329-5276
Exeter: Suicide Support 603-778-7391
Keene: Safe Place/The Samaritans of Keene 603-357-5505
Manchester: Survivors of Suicide 603-644-2525

New Jersey

Dumont: Survivors After Suicide 201-385-4400
Madison: Survivors of Suicide 201-786-5178
Piscataway: Survivors of Suicide 908-235-4109
Toms River: Survivors of Suicide 908-505-5437

New Mexico

Albuquerque: Survivors of Suicide 505-858-1240

New York

Albany: Safe Place/The Samaritans of the Capital
District 518-459-0196

Babylon: Compassionate Friends/Parents of Suicide
516-661-7012
Brooklyn: Ray of Hope 718-738-9217
Buffalo: Suicide Bereavement Group 716-685-2733
Douglaston (Queens): Survivors of Suicide Support
Group 516-466-8423
Flushing (Queens): Survivors of Suicide 718-463-1639
Ithaca: After Suicide Support Group 607-272-1505;
607-272-1616
Massapequa: South Shore Suicide Survivors Group
516-798-7881
Manhattan: Safe Place/The Samaritans of New York
212-673-3000
Port Jefferson: Survivors of Suicide 516-474-6061
Rochester: After Suicide 716-654-7262
Roslyn Heights: Survivors After the Suicide of a Loved
One 516-626-1971
Staten Island: Survivors of Suicide 718-448-3306
White Plains: C.A.R.E.S. 914-997-5849

North Carolina

Mount Airy: Survivors of Suicide 910-789-5108

North Dakota

Bismarck: Grief After Suicide 800-472-2911; 701-255-3692
Fargo: Suicide Survivor Support Group 701-293-6462
Grand Forks: Survivors of Suicide 701-795-3000
Minot: Survivors of Suicide 701-857-2230
Wahpeton: Suicide Survivor Support Group
701-293-6462

Ohio

Akron: Survivors 216-253-9388
Canton: Survivors of Suicide 216-452-6000
Cincinnati: Survivors After Suicide 513-385-6110
Cincinnati: Survivors of Suicide 513-841-1012
Columbus: Survivors of Suicide 614-279-9382
Dayton: Survivors of Suicide 513-297-9096
Delaware: Helpline 800-684-2324
Lakewood: Survivors of Suicide 216-521-1335
Toledo: Survivors of Suicide 419-385-9205
Westerville: Survivors of Suicide 614-882-9338
Youngstown: Survivors of Suicide Support Group
216-747-5111

Oklahoma

Norman: Survivors of Suicide 405-329-4280
Oklahoma City: Survivors of Suicide 405-942-1345
Tulsa: Survivors of Suicide 918-585-1213

Oregon

Albany: Survivors of Suicide Support Group
503-394-3707
Medford: Healing from Suicide 503-772-2527
Portland: Suicide Bereavement Support 503-657-1181

Pennsylvania

Altoona: Support Group for Those Who Have Lost a
Loved One Through Suicide 814-946-2209
Butler: Survivors of Suicide 412-287-1965
Fort Washington: Survivors of Suicide 215-545-2242
Lancaster: Survivors of Suicide 717-898-8239
Langhorne: Survivors of Suicide 215-545-2242

Levittown: Survivors of Suicide 215-545-2242
Lewisburg: Survivors of Suicide 717-523-7509
Monaca: Suicide's Other Victims 412-775-4165
Philadelphia: Survivors of Suicide 215-545-2242
Philadelphia: Survivors of Suicide 215-745-8247
Pittsburgh: Survivors of Suicide 412-624-5170
Quakertown: Survivors of Suicide 215-536-5143
Wilkes-Barre: Survivors of Suicide 717-822-7118

Rhode Island

Providence: Safe Place/The Samaritans of Rhode Island
401-272-4044

South Carolina

Anderson: Survivors of Suicide 864-646-5167
Charleston: Survivors of Suicide 803-744-4357
Columbia: Survivors of Suicide 803-356-2874
Greenville: Survivors of Suicide Support Group
864-271-8888

South Dakota

Sioux Falls: Survivors of Suicide 605-336-1974

Tennessee

Chattanooga: Living After Suicide 423-875-2509
Nashville: Survivors of Suicide Support Group
615-244-7444

Texas

Amarillo: Surviving Connection 806-342-3600
Corpus Christi: Survivors After Suicide 512-853-1964
Dallas: Survivors of Suicide Support Group 214-828-1000
Ft Worth: Survivors of Suicide 817-654-5343
Houston: Survivors of Suicide 713-228-1505
Lubbock: Survivors of Suicide 806-765-7272
Lufkin: Survivors of Suicide 409-632-1514
Midland: Survivors of Suicide Support Group
915-685-1566
Plano: Survivors of Suicide 214-881-0088
San Angelo: Heartbeat 915-944-1666
San Antonio: S.O.L.O.S. 210-695-9136

Utah

Layton: Legacy 801-771-8476
Park City: SEASONS: Suicide Bereavement 801-649-8327

Vermont

There are no groups currently in the state of Vermont

Virginia

Falls Church: Suicide Survivors Support Group
703-273-3454
Hopewell: Healing After Suicide 804-458-3895
Newport News: Survivors of Suicide Support Group
757-875-0060
Portsmouth: Survivors of Suicide Support Group
804-483-5111
Richmond: Surviving 804-780-6911
Virginia Beach: Survivors of Suicide 757-469-6000

Winchester: Survivors of Suicide Support Group
540-667-1178

Washington

Auburn: Survivors of Suicide 206-833-7127
Kennewick: Survivors of Suicide 509-783-7416
Seattle: Survivors of Suicide 206-461-3222
Seattle: Survivors of Suicide 206-772-5141
Spokane: Survivors of a Loved One's Suicide
509-483-3310
Tacoma: Survivors of Suicide 206-474-3330

West Virginia

Huntington: Heartbeat 304-526-6001
Wheeling: Survivors of Suicide Support Group
304-277-3916

Wisconsin

Appleton: Fox Valley Survivors of Suicide 414-739-1231
Eau Claire: Suicide Survivors Support Group
715-833-6028
La Crosse: Karis Support Group 608-785-0530, ext. 3652
Madison: Survivors of Suicide 608-251-2345
Marshfield: Survivors of Suicide 715-387-7753
Milwaukee: Survivors Helping Survivors 414-649-6000,
ext. 6230
Sheboygan: Suicide Loss Support Group 414-458-3951
Wisconsin Rapids: Survivors of Suicide 715-421-1942

Wyoming

Cheyenne: Share and Care 307-637-3753

ABOUT THE AUTHOR

Steve Sorensen was born in Colorado Springs, Colorado. He has worked as a software developer for over twenty years. His first book, "Surviving My Son's Suicide: A Father's Perspective" was born out of the deep desire to understand what brought his twenty-year-old son to suicide. Steve lives and works in Denver, Colorado with his wife and two children.